A NEW PHILOSOPHY OF SOCIETY

Also Avaliable from Continuum

Intensive Science and Virtual Philosophy – Manuel DeLanda

A NEW PHILOSOPHY OF SOCIETY

Assemblage Theory and Social Complexity

Manuel DeLanda

continuum

Continuum

The Tower Building
11 York Road
London, SE1 7NX

80 Maiden Lane
Suite 704
New York, NY 10038

www.continuumbooks.com

First published 2006
Reprinted 2007 (twice)

British Library Cataloguing-in-Publication Data
A catalogue record for this book is available from the British Library

ISBN-10: 0-8264-8170-1 (hardback) 0-8264-9169-3 (paperback)
ISBN-13: 978-0-8264-8170-2 (hardback) 978-0-8264-9169-5 (paperback)

Library of Congress Cataloging-in-Publication Data
A catalog record for this book is available from the Library of Congress

Typeset by BookEns Ltd, Royston, Herts.
Printed and bound in Great Britain by Biddles Ltd.,
King's Lynn, Norfolk

Contents

Introduction

The purpose of this book is to introduce a novel approach to social ontology. Like any other ontological investigation it concerns itself with the question of what kinds of entities we can legitimately commit ourselves to assert exist. The ontological stance taken here has traditionally been labelled 'realist': a stance usually defined by a commitment to the mind-independent existence of reality. In the case of social ontology, however, this definition must be qualified because most social entities, from small communities to large nation-states, would disappear altogether if human minds ceased to exist. In this sense social entities are clearly not mind-independent. Hence, a realist approach to social ontology must assert the autonomy of social entities from the conceptions we have of them. To say that social entities have a reality that is conception-independent is simply to assert that the theories, models and classifications we use to study them may be objectively wrong, that is, that they may fail to capture the real history and internal dynamics of those entities.

There are, however, important cases in which the very models and classifications social scientists use affect the behaviour of the entities being studied. Political or medical classifications using categories like 'female refugee' or 'hyperactive child', for example, may interact with the people being classified if they become aware of the fact that they are being so classified. In the first case, a woman fleeing terrible conditions in her home country may become aware of the criteria to classify 'female refugees' used by the country to which she wants to emigrate, and change her behaviour to fit that criteria. In this case, an ontological commitment to the referent of the term 'female refugee' would be hard to maintain, since the very use of the term may be creating its own referents. On the other hand, accepting that the referents of some general terms may in fact be moving targets does not undermine social realism: to explain the case of the female refugee one has to invoke, in addition to her awareness of the meaning of the term 'female refugee', the objective existence of a whole set of institutional organizations (courts, immigration agencies, airports and seaports, detention centres), institutional norms and objects (laws, binding court decisions, passports) and institutional practices (confining, monitoring, interrogating), forming the context in which the interactions between categories and their referents take place. In other words, the problem for a realist social ontology arises here *not* because the meanings of all general terms shape the very perception that social scientists have of their referents, creating a vicious circle, but only in some special cases and in the context of institutions and practices that are not reducible to meanings. As the philosopher Ian Hacking writes:

> I do not necessarily mean that hyperactive children, as individuals, on their own, become aware of how they are classified, and thus react to the classification. Of course they may, but the interaction occurs in the larger matrix of institutions and practices surrounding this classification. There was a time when children described as hyperactive were placed in 'stim-free' classrooms: classrooms in which stimuli were minimized, so that children would have no occasion for excess activity. Desks were far apart. The walls had no decoration. The windows were curtained. The teacher wore a plain black dress with no ornaments. The walls were designed for minimum noise reflection. The classification *hyperactive* did not interact with the children simply because individual children had heard the word and changed accordingly. It interacted with those who were so described in institutions and practices that were predicated upon classifying children that way.[1]

In short, acknowledging the existence of troublesome cases in which the meanings of words affect their own referents in no way compromises a realist approach to institutions and practices. On the contrary, a correct solution to this problem seems to demand an ontology in which the existence of institutional organizations, interpersonal networks and many other social entities is treated as conception-independent. This realist solution is diametrically opposed to the idealist one espoused by phenomenologically influenced sociologists, the so-called 'social constructivists'. In fact, as Hacking points out, these sociologists use the term 'construction' in a purely metaphorical sense, ignoring 'its literal meaning, that of building or assembling from parts'.[2] By contrast, the realist social ontology to be defended in this book is all about objective processes of assembly: a wide range of social entities, from persons to nation-states, will be treated as assemblages constructed through very specific historical processes, processes in which language plays an important but not a constitutive role.

A theory of assemblages, and of the processes that create and stabilize their historical identity, was created by the philosopher Gilles Deleuze in the last decades of the twentieth century. This theory was meant to apply to a wide variety of wholes constructed from heterogeneous parts. Entities ranging from atoms and molecules to biological organisms, species and ecosystems may be usefully treated as assemblages and therefore as entities that are products of historical processes. This implies, of course, that one uses the term 'historical' to include cosmological and evolutionary history, not only human history. Assemblage theory may also be applied to social entities, but the very fact that it cuts across the nature–culture divide is evidence of its realist credentials. It may be objected, however, that the relatively few pages dedicated to assemblage theory in the work of Deleuze (much of it in partnership with Félix Guattari) hardly amount to a fully-fledged theory.[3] And this is, in fact, correct. But the concepts used to specify the characteristics of assemblages in those few pages (concepts such as 'expression' or 'territorialization') are highly elaborated and connected to yet other concepts throughout Deleuze's work. Taking into account the entire network of ideas within which the concept of 'assemblage' performs its conceptual duties, we do have at least the rudiments of a theory. But this, in turn, raises another difficulty. The definitions of the concepts used to characterize assemblages are dispersed throughout Deleuze's work: part of a definition may be in one book, extended somewhere else, and qualified later in some obscure essay. Even in those cases where conceptual definitions are easy to locate, they are usually not given in a style that allows for a straightforward interpretation. This would seem to condemn a book on assemblage theory to spend most of its pages doing hermeneutics.

To sidestep this difficulty I have elsewhere reconstructed the whole of

Deleuzian ontology, including those parts that bear directly on assemblage theory, in a clear, analytic style that makes a preoccupation with what Deleuze 'really meant' almost completely unnecessary.[4] In this book I will make use of a similar strategy: I will give my own definitions of the technical terms, use my own arguments to justify them, and use entirely different theoretical resources to develop them. This manœuvre will not completely eliminate the need to engage in Deleuzian hermeneutics but it will allow me to confine that part of the job to footnotes. Readers who feel that the theory developed here is not strictly speaking Deleuze's own are welcome to call it 'neo-assemblage theory', 'assemblage theory 2.0', or some other name.

The first two chapters of this book introduce the fundamental ideas of such a reconstructed theory of assemblages. This theory must, first of all, account for the *synthesis* of the properties of a whole not reducible to its parts. In this synthetic function assemblage theory has rivals that are historically much older, such as Hegelian dialectics. Thus, an important task, one to be carried out in Chapter 1, is to contrast assemblages and Hegelian totalities. The main difference is that in assemblage theory the fact that a whole possess synthetic or emergent properties does not preclude the possibility of analysis. In other words, unlike organic totalities, the parts of an assemblage do not form a seamless whole. In Chapter 2 I will argue that once historical processes are used to explain the synthesis of inorganic, organic and social assemblages there is no need for essentialism to account for their enduring identities. This allows assemblage theory to avoid one of the main shortcomings of other forms of social realism: an ontological commitment to the existence of essences.

Once the basic ideas have been laid out, the next three chapters apply the assemblage approach to a concrete case-study: the problem of the link between the micro- and the macro-levels of social reality. Traditionally, this problem has been framed in reductionist terms. Reductionism in social science is often illustrated with the methodological individualism characteristic of microeconomics, in which all that matters are rational decisions made by individual persons in isolation from one another. But the phenomenological individualism of social constructivism is also reductionist even though its conception of the micro-level is not based on individual rationality but on the routines and categories that structure individual experience. In neither one of these individualisms is there a denial that there exists, in addition to rationality or experience, something like 'society as a whole'. But such an entity is conceptualized as a mere aggregate, that is, as a whole without properties that are more than the sum of its parts. For this reason we may refer to these solutions to the micro–macro problem as 'micro-reductionist'.

The other position that has been historically adopted towards the micro–macro problem is that social structure is what really exists, individual persons being mere products of the society in which they are born. The young Durkheim, the older Marx, and functionalists such as Talcott Parsons are examples of this stance. These authors do not deny the existence of individual persons but assume that once they have been socialized by the family and the school, they have so internalized the values of the societies or the social classes to which they belong that their allegiance to a given social order may be taken for granted. This tends to make the micro-level a mere epiphenomenon and for this reason this stance may be labelled 'macro-reductionist'. There are many other positions taken in social science towards the problem of the articulation of the micro and the macro, including making an intermediate level, such as praxis, the true core of social reality, with both individual agency and social structure being byproducts of this fundamental level. This seems to be the stance taken by such prominent contemporary sociologists as Anthony Giddens, a stance that may be labelled 'meso-reductionist'.[5]

These three reductionist positions do not, of course, exhaust the possibilities. There are many social scientists whose work focuses on social entities that are neither micro nor macro: Erving Goffman's work on conversations and other social encounters; Max Weber's work on institutional organizations; Charles Tilly's work on social justice movements; not to mention the large number of sociologists working on the theory of social networks, or the geographers studying cities and regions. What the work of these authors reveals is a large number of intermediate levels between the micro and the macro, the ontological status of which has not been properly conceptualized. Assemblage theory can provide the framework in which the contributions of these and other authors (including the work of those holding reductionist stances) may be properly located and the connections between them fully elucidated. This is because assemblages, being wholes whose properties emerge from the interactions between parts, can be used to model any of these intermediate entities: interpersonal networks and institutional organizations are assemblages of people; social justice movements are assemblages of several networked communities; central governments are assemblages of several organizations; cities are assemblages of people, networks, organizations, as well as of a variety of infrastructural components, from buildings and streets to conduits for matter and energy flows; nation-states are assemblages of cities, the geographical regions organized by cities, and the provinces that several such regions form.

Chapters 3, 4 and 5 take the reader on a journey that, starting at the personal (and even subpersonal) scale, climbs up one scale at a time all the way to territorial states and beyond. It is only by experiencing this upward movement, the movement that in reality generates all these emergent wholes, that a reader can get a sense of the irreducible social complexity characterizing the contemporary world. This does not imply that the ontological scheme proposed here is not applicable to simpler or older societies: it can be used in truncated form to apply it to societies without cities or large central governments, for example. I make, on the other hand, no effort to be multicultural: all my examples come from either Europe or the USA. This simply reflects my belief that some of the properties of social assemblages, such as interpersonal networks or institutional organizations, remain approximately invariant across different cultures. But even the illustrations from Western nations are often sketchy and, with the exception of Chapter 5, the historical aspects of my examples are not fully explored. This shortcoming is justified by the fact that my older publications have already engaged history and historical dynamics, and that in this book I am exclusively interested in a clarification of the ontological status of the entities that are the actors of my earlier historical narratives.[6] The shortage of historical examples is also intended to reduce the time the reader spends at each level of scale, that is, to increase the speed of the upward movement, since for this book it is the reader's experience of the journey from the micro to the macro that matters the most. It is my hope that once the complexity of that forgotten territory between the micro and the macro is grasped at visceral level, the intellectual habit to privilege one or the other extreme will become easier to break.

On the other hand, a solution to the micro–macro problem in terms of a multiplicity of social entities operating at intermediate levels of scale calls for a few words to clarify the meaning of the expression 'larger-scale'. Its usual meaning is geometric, as when when one says that a street is the longest one in a city, or that one nation-state occupies a larger area than another. But there is also a physical meaning of the expression that goes beyond geometry. In physics, for example, length, area and volume are classified as *extensive* properties, a category that also includes amount of energy and number of components. It is in this latter extensive sense, not the geometric one, that I use the expression 'larger-scale'. Two interpersonal networks, for example, will be compared in scale by the number of members they contain not by the extent of the geographical area they occupy, so that a network structuring a local community will be said to be larger than one linking geographically dispersed friends if it has more members, regardless of the fact that the latter may span the entire planet. Also, being larger in only one of the properties differentiating the social entities to be discussed here. There are many others properties (such as the density of the connections in a network, or the degree of centralization of authority in an organization) that are not extensive but *intensive*, and that are equally important. Finally, social entities will be characterized in this book not only by their properties but also by their capacities, that is, by what they are capable of doing when they interact with other social entities.

To those readers who may be disappointed by the lack of cross-cultural comparisons, or the absence of detailed analyses of social mechanisms, or the poverty of the historical vignettes, I can only say that none of these worthy tasks can be really carried out within an impoverished ontological framework. When social scientists pretend to be able to perform these tasks without ontological foundations, they are typically using an implicit, and thereby uncritically accepted, ontology. There is simply no way out of this dilemma. Thus, while philosophers cannot, and should not, pretend to do the work of social scientists for them, they can greatly contribute to the job of ontological clarification. This is the task that this book attempts to perform.

Manuel DeLanda
New York, 2005

1
Assemblages against Totalities

The purpose of this chapter is to introduce the theory of assemblages. But this introduction is not meant as an end in itself, but as a means to elucidate the proper ontological status of the entities that are invoked by sociologists and other social scientists. Is there, for example, such a thing as society as a whole? Is the commitment to assert the existence of such an entity legitimate? And, is denying the reality of such an entity equivalent to a commitment to the existence of only individual persons and their families? The answer to all these questions is a definitive no, but several obstacles must be removed before justifying this negative response. Of all the obstacles standing in the way of an adequate social ontology none is as entrenched as the *organismic metaphor*. In its least sophisticated form this stumbling-block involves making a superficial analogy between society and the human body, and to postulate that just as bodily organs work together for the organism as a whole, so the function of social institutions is to work in harmony for the benefit of society. As historians of social thought Howard Becker and Harry Barnes have noted, there are many variants of this centuries-old metaphor, some more sophisticated than others:

> The theory of the resemblance between classes, groups, and institutions in society and the organs of the individual is as old as social theory itself. We have already noted its presence in Hindu social thought, and have also called attention to the fact that Aristotle, in book IV of his Politics, sets forth this organismic analogy with precision and clarity. The same conception appears clearly in the writings of

ASSEMBLAGES AGAINST TOTALITIES

Cicero, Livy, Seneca, and Paul. In the Middle Ages elaborate anthropomorphic analogies were drawn by John of Salisbury and Nicholas of Cues. In the early modern period, Hobbes and Rousseau contrasted the organism and the state, holding that the organism was the product of nature while the state was an artificial creation. In the late eighteenth and early nineteenth century fanciful notions of the social and political organism appeared with such writers as Hegel, Schelling, Krause, Ahrens, Schmitthenner, and Waitz.[1]

In the late nineteenth century the organismic metaphor achieved its first systematic development in the work of Herbert Spencer and reached its pinnacle of influence a few decades later in the work of Talcott Parsons, the most important figure of the functionalist school of sociology. After this, the use of the organism as a metaphor declined as sociologists rejected functionalism, some because of its emphasis on social integration and its disregard for conflict, others because of its focus on social structure at the expense of phenomenological experience. But a more sophisticated form of the basic metaphor still exerts considerable influence in most schools of sociology, and in this form it is much more difficult to eliminate. This version involves not an analogy but a general theory about the relations between parts and wholes, wholes that constitute a seamless totality or that display an organic unity. The basic concept in this theory is what we may call *relations of interiority*: the component parts are constituted by the very relations they have to other parts in the whole. A part detached from such a whole ceases to be what it is, since being this particular part is one of its constitutive properties. A whole in which the component parts are self-subsistent and their relations are external to each other does not possess an organic unity. As Hegel wrote: 'This is what constitutes the character of mechanism, namely, that whatever relation obtains between the things combined, this relation is *extraneous* to them that does not concern their nature at all, and even if it is accompanied by a semblance of unity it remains nothing more than *composition, mixture, aggregation*, and the like.'[2]

Thus, in this conception wholes possess an inextricable unity in which there is a strict reciprocal determination between parts. This version of organismic theory is much harder to eliminate because it is not just a matter of rejecting an old worn-out image and because its impact on sociology goes beyond functionalism. A good contemporary example is the work of the influential sociologist Anthony Giddens, who attempts to transcend the duality of agency and structure by arguing for their mutual constitution: agency is constituted by its involvement in practice which, in turn, reproduces structure. Structure is conceived as consisting of behavioural procedures and routines, and of material and symbolic resources, neither one of which possesses a separate existence outside of their instantiation in actual practice.[3] In turn, the practices which instantiate rules and mobilize resources are conceived by Giddens as a continuous flow of action 'not composed of an aggregate or series of separate intentions, reasons, and motives'.[4] The end result of this is a seamless whole in which agency and structure mutually constitute one another dialectically.[5]

Following Hegel, other defenders of this approach argue that without relations of interiority a whole cannot have emergent properties, becoming a mere aggregation of the properties of its components. It may be argued, however, that a whole may be both analysable into separate parts and at the same time have irreducible properties, properties that emerge from the *interactions* between parts. As the philosopher of science Mario Bunge remarks, the 'possibility of analysis does not entail reduction, and explanation of the mechanisms of emergence does not explain emergence away'.[6] Allowing the possibility of complex interactions between component parts is crucial to define mechanisms of emergence, but this possibility disappears if the parts are fused together into a seamless web. Thus, what needs to be challenged is the very idea of relations of interiority. We can distinguish, for example, the properties defining a given entity from its *capacities to interact* with other entities. While its properties are given and may be denumerable as a closed list, its capacities are not given – they may go unexercised if no entity suitable for interaction is around – and form a potentially open list, since there is no way to tell in advance in what way a given entity may affect or be affected by innumerable other entities. In this other view, being part of a whole involves the exercise of a part's capacities but it is not a constitutive property of it. And given that an unexercised capacity does not affect what a component is, a part may be detached from the whole while preserving its identity.

Today, the main theoretical alternative to organic totalities is what the philosopher Gilles Deleuze calls *assemblages*, wholes characterized by *relations of exteriority*. These relations imply, first of all, that a component part of an assemblage may be detached from it and plugged into a different assemblage in which its interactions are different. In other words, the exteriority of relations implies a certain autonomy for the terms they relate, or as Deleuze puts it, it implies that 'a relation may change without the terms changing'.[7] Relations of exteriority also imply that the properties of the component parts can never explain the relations which constitute a whole, that is, 'relations do not have as their causes the properties of the [component parts] between which they are established ...'[8] although they may be caused by the exercise of a component's capacities. In fact, the reason why the properties of a whole cannot be reduced to those of its parts is that they are the result not of an aggregation of the components' own properties but of the actual exercise of their capacities. These capacities do depend on a component's properties but cannot be reduced to them since they involve reference to the properties of other interacting entities. Relations of exteriority guarantee that assemblages may be taken apart while at the same time allowing that the interactions between parts may result in a true synthesis.

While those favouring the interiority of relations tend to use organisms as their prime example, Deleuze gravitates towards other kinds of biological illustrations, such as the symbiosis of plants and pollinating insects. In this case we have relations of exteriority between self-subsistent components – such as the wasp and the orchid – relations which may become obligatory in the course of coevolution. This illustrates another difference between assemblages and totalities. A seamless whole is inconceivable except as a synthesis of these very parts, that is, the linkages between its components form *logically necessary* relations which make the whole what it is. But in an assemblage these relations may be only *contingently obligatory*. While logically necessary relations may be investigated by thought alone, contingently obligatory ones involve a consideration of empirical questions, such as the coevolutionary history of two species. In addition to this Deleuze considers heterogeneity of components an important characteristic of assemblages. Thus, he would consider ecosystems as assemblages of thousands of different plant and animal species, but not the species themselves, since natural selection tends to homogenize their gene pools. In what follows I will not take heterogeneity as a constant property of assemblages but as a variable that may take different values. This will allow me to consider not only species but also biological organisms as assemblages, instead of having to introduce another category for them as does Deleuze.[9] Conceiving an organism as an assemblage implies that despite the tight integration between its component organs, the relations between them are not logically necessary but only contingently obligatory: a historical result of their close coevolution. In this way assemblage theory deprives organismic theories of their most cherished exemplar.

In addition to the exteriority of relations, the concept of assemblage is defined along two dimensions. One dimension or axis defines the variable roles which an assemblage's components may play, from a purely *material* role at one extreme of the axis, to a purely *expressive* role at the other extreme. These roles are variable and may occur in mixtures, that is, a given component may play a mixture of material and expressive roles by exercising different sets of capacities. The other dimension defines variable processes in which these components become involved and that either stabilize the identity of an assemblage, by increasing its degree of internal homogeneity or the degree of sharpness of its boundaries, or destabilize it. The former are referred to as processes of *territorialization* and the latter as processes of *deterritorialization*.[10] One and the same assemblage can have components working to stabilize its identity as well as components forcing it to change or even transforming it into a different assemblage. In fact, one and the same component may participate in both processes by exercising different sets of capacities. Let me give some simple social examples of these four variables.

The components of social assemblages playing a material role vary widely, but at the very least involve a set of human bodies properly oriented (physically or psychologically) towards each other. The classic example of these assemblages of bodies is face-to-face conversations, but the interpersonal networks that structure communities, as well as the hierarchical organizations that govern cities or nation-states, can also serve as illustrations. Community networks and institutional organizations are assemblages of bodies, but they also possess a variety of other material components, from food and physical labour, to simple tools and complex machines, to the buildings and neighbourhoods serving as their physical locales. Illustrating the components playing an expressive role needs some elaboration because in assemblage theory expressivity cannot be reduced to language and symbols. A main component of conversations is, of course, the content of the talk, but there are also many forms of bodily expression (posture, dress, facial gestures) that are not linguistic. In addition, there is what participants express about themselves not by what they say but by the way they say it, or even by their very choice of topic.

These are nonlinguistic social expressions which matter from the point of view of a person's reputation (or the image he or she tries to project in conversations) as much as what the person expresses linguistically. Similarly, an important component of an interpersonal network is the expressions of solidarity of its members, but these can be either linguistic (promises, vows) or behavioural, the solidarity expressed by shared sacrifice or mutual help even in the absence of words. Hierarchical organizations, in turn, depend on expressions of legitimacy, which may be embodied linguistically (in the form of beliefs about the sources of authority) or in the behaviour of their members, in the sense that the very act of obeying commands in public, in the absence of physical coercion, expresses acceptance of legitimate authority.[11]

The concept of territorialization must be first of all understood literally. Face-to-face conversations always occur in a particular place (a street-corner, a pub, a church), and once the participants have ratified one another a conversation acquires well-defined spatial boundaries. Similarly, many interpersonal networks define communities inhabiting spatial territories, whether ethnic neighbourhoods or small towns, with well-defined borders. Organizations, in turn, usually operate in particular buildings, and the jurisdiction of their legitimate authority usually coincides with the physical boundaries of those buildings. The exceptions are governmental organizations, but in this case too their jurisdictional boundaries tend to be geographical: the borders of a town, a province or a whole country. So, in the first place, processes of territorialization are processes that define or sharpen the spatial boundaries of actual territories. Territorialization, on the other hand, also refers to non-spatial processes which increase the internal homogeneity of an assemblage, such as the sorting processes which exclude a certain category of people from membership of an organization, or the segregation processes which increase the ethnic or racial homogeneity of a neighbourhood. Any process which either destabilizes spatial boundaries or increases internal heterogeneity is considered deterritorializing. A good example is communication technology, ranging from writing and a reliable postal service, to telegraphs, telephones and computers, all of which blur the spatial boundaries of social entities by eliminating the need for co-presence: they enable conversations to take place at a distance, allow interpersonal networks to form via regular correspondence, phone calls or computer communications, and give organizations the means to operate in different countries at the same time.

While the decomposition of an assemblage into its different parts, and the assignment of a material or expressive role to each component, exemplifies the analytic side of the approach, the concept of territorialization plays a synthetic role, since it is in part through the more or less permanent articulations produced by this process that a whole emerges from its parts and maintains its identity once it has emerged. But there is another synthetic process in assemblage theory that complements territorialization: the role played in the production and maintenance of identity by specialized expressive entities such as genes and words. Although Deleuze considers all entities, even nonbiological and nonsocial ones, as being capable of expression, he argues that the historical appearance of these specialized entities allowed a great complexification of the kinds of wholes that could be assembled in this planet. Let me elaborate this point starting with the idea that physical or chemical entities are capable of expression. When atoms interact with radiation their internal structure creates patterns in this radiation through the selective absorption of some of its wavelengths. In manmade photographs this pattern appears as a spatial arrangement of light and dark bands (a spectrograph) which is correlated in a unique way with the identity of the chemical species to which the atom belongs. In other words, the absorption pattern *expresses the identity* of the chemical species in the form of physical information which can be used by astrophysicists, for example, to identify the chemical elements present in a given celestial process.[12]

On the other hand, this expressivity is clearly not functional in any sense. That is, while the information patterns do have an objective existence, in the absence of astrophysicists (or other users of spectrographs) the patterns do not perform any function. These patterns may be compared to the fingerprints that are expressive of human organic identity, but that in the absence of a law-enforcement organization that collects them, stores them and retrieves them as part of a process of identification, perform no real biological function at all. But, Deleuze argues, there have been critical thresholds in the history of the planet when physical expressivity has become functional. The first threshold is the emergence of the genetic code, marking the point at which information patterns ceased to depend on the full three-dimensional structure of an entity (such as that of an atom) and became a separate one-dimensional structure, a long chain of nucleic acids. The second threshold is the emergence of language: while genetic linearity is still linked to spatial relations of contiguity, linguistic vocalizations display a *temporal linearity* that endows its information patterns with an even greater autonomy from their material carrier.[13] These two specialized lines of expression must be considered assemblages in their own right. Like all assemblages they exhibit a part-to-whole relation: genes are made up of linear sequences of nucleotides, and are the component parts of chromosomes; words are made of linear sequences of phonetic sounds or written letters, and are the component parts of sentences. Some of these component parts play a material role, a physical substratum for the information, and through elaborate mechanisms this information can be expressed as proteins, in the case of genetic materials, or as meanings, in the case of linguistic ones.[14]

In assemblage theory, these two specialized expressive media are viewed as the basis for a second synthetic process. While territorialization provides a first articulation of the components, the *coding* performed by genes or words supplies a second articulation, consolidating the effects of the first and further stabilizing the identity of assemblages.[15] Biological organisms are examples of assemblages synthesized through both territorialization and coding, but so are many social entities, such as hierarchical organizations. The coding process in the latter will vary depending on whether the source of legitimate authority in these hierarchies is traditional or rational–legal, as in modern bureaucracies. In the former the coding is performed by narratives establishing the sacred origins of authority, while in the latter it is effected by constitutions spelling out the rights and obligations associated with each formal role. It is tempting to see in the fact that both biological organisms and some of the most visible social institutions are doubly articulated, the source of the appeal of the organismic metaphor: the isomorphism of the processes giving rise to some biological and social entities would explain their resemblance. On the other hand, this real resemblance should not license the idea that 'society as a whole' is like an organism, since many social assemblages are not highly coded or highly territorialized.

In fact, in both the biological and the social realms there are processes of *decoding*, yielding assemblages which do not conform to the organismic metaphor. In biology such decoding is illustrated by animal behaviour which has ceased to be rigidly programmed by genes to be learned from experience in a more flexible way. This decoding produces, for example, animal territories, the assemblages generated when animals have gone beyond the passive expression of information patterns (patterns of the fingerprint kind) actively to use a variety of means – from faeces and urine to song, colour and silhouette – as an expression of their identity as owners of a particular geographical area.[16] A social example of the result of a process of decoding would be informal conversations between friends. As social assemblages, conversations do not have the same durability of either interpersonal networks or institutional organizations, and no one would feel tempted to compare them to organisms. But they do involve rules, such as those governing turn-taking. The more formal and rigid the rules, the more these social encounters may be said to be coded. But in some circumstances these rules may be weakened giving rise to assemblages in which the participants have more room to express their convictions and their own personal styles.[17]

Nevertheless, and despite the importance of genetic and linguistic components for the consolidation of the identity of biological and social assemblages, it is crucial not to conceptualize their links to other components as relations of interiority. In other words, the interactions of genes with the rest of a body's machinery should not be viewed as if they constituted the defining essence of that machinery. And similarly for the interactions of language with subjective experience or with social institutions. In an assemblage approach, genes and words are simply one more component entering into relations of exteriority with a variety of other material and expressive components, and the processes of coding and decoding based on these specialized lines of expression operate side by side with nongenetic and nonlinguistic processes of territorialization and deterritorialization. To emphasize this point in the chapters that follow, I will always discuss language last and as a separate component. This will allow me to distinguish clearly those expressive components that are not linguistic but which are mistakenly treated as if they were symbolic, as well as to emphasize that language should be moved away from the core of the matter, a place that it has wrongly occupied for many decades now.

There are two more questions that must be discussed to complete the characterization of the assemblage approach. The first regards the processes of assembly though which physical, biological and social entities come into being, processes that must be conceptualized as *recurrent*. This implies that assemblages always exist in *populations*, however small, the populations generated by the repeated occurrence of the same processes. As the assemblages making up these collectivities interact with one another, exercising a variety of capacities, these interactions endow the populations with some properties of their own, such as a certain rate of growth or certain average distributions of assemblage properties. The second question regards the possibility that within these collectivities larger assemblages may emerge of which the members of the population are the component parts. In other words, the interactions between members of a collectivity may lead to the formation of more or less permanent articulations between them yielding a macro-assemblage with properties and capacities of its own. Since the processes behind the formation of these enduring articulations are themselves recurrent, a population of larger assemblages will be created leading to the possibility of even larger ones emerging.

The combination of recurrence of the same assembly processes at any one spatial scale, and the recurrence of the same kind of assembly processes (territorialization and coding) at successive scales, gives assemblage theory a unique way of approaching the problem of linking the micro- and macro-levels of social reality. The bulk of this book will be spent giving concrete examples of how we can bridge the level of individual persons and that of the largest social entities (such as territorial states) through an embedding of assemblages in a succession of micro- and macro-scales. But at this point it will prove useful to give a simple illustration. One advantage of the present approach is that it allows the replacement of vaguely defined general entities (like 'the market' or 'the state') with concrete assemblages. What would replace, for example, 'the market' in an assemblage approach? Markets should be viewed, first of all, as concrete organizations (that is, concrete market-places or bazaars) and this fact makes them assemblages made out of people and the material and expressive goods people exchange.

In addition, as the economic historian Fernand Braudel argues, these organizations must be located in a concrete physical locale, such as a small town and its surrounding countryside, a locale which should also be considered a component of the assemblage. In these terms, the smallest economic assemblage has always been, as Braudel says:

a complex consisting of a small market town, perhaps the site of a fair, with a cluster of dependent villages around it. Each village had to be close enough to the town for it to be possible to go to the market and back in a day. But the actual dimensions of the unit would equally depend on the available means of transport, the density of settlement and the fertility of the area in question.[18]

Roughly, prior to the emergence of steam-driven transport, the average size of these complexes varied between 160 and 170 square kilometres. In the high Middle Ages, as European urbanization intensified, these local markets multiplied, generating a large population of similar assemblages. Then, some of the market-places belonging to these population were assembled together into *regional markets*, larger assemblages with an average area of 1,500 to 1,700 square kilometres. Each such region typically exhibited a dominant city as its centre and a recognizable cultural identity, both of which are parts of the larger assemblage. Next came *provincial markets*, with dimensions about ten times as large as the regional markets they assembled, but a lesser degree of internal homogeneity.[19] Finally, when several such provincial markets were stitched together, as they were in England in the eighteenth century, *national markets* emerged.

This brief description yields a very clear picture of a series of differently scaled assemblages, some of which are component parts of others which, in turn, become parts of even larger ones. Although I left out the historical details behind the assembly of local market-places into regional markets, or those behind the creation of national markets, it is clear that in each case there was a process through which larger entities emerged from the assembly of smaller ones. As Braudel notes of national markets, they were 'a network of irregular weave, often constructed against all odds: against the over-powerful cities with their own policies, against the provinces which resisted centralization, against foreign intervention which breached frontiers, not to mention the divergent interests of production and exchange'.[20] The situation is, indeed, even more complex because I am leaving out long-distance trade and the international markets to which this type of trade gave rise. But even this simplified picture is already infinitely better than the reified generality of 'the market'.

Let me summarize the main features of assemblage theory. First of all, unlike wholes in which parts are linked by relations of interiority (that is, relations which constitute the very identity of the parts) assemblages are made up of parts which are self-subsistent and articulated by relations of exteriority, so that a part may be detached and made a component of another assemblage. Assemblages are characterized along two dimensions: along the first dimension are specified the variable roles which component parts may play, from a purely material role to a purely expressive one, as well as mixtures of the two. A second dimension characterizes processes in which these components are involved: processes which stabilize or destabilize the identity of the assemblage (territorialization and deterritorialization). In the version of assemblage theory to be used in this book, a third dimension will be added: an extra axis defining processes in which specialized expressive media intervene, processes which consolidate and rigidify the identity of the assemblage or, on the contrary, allow the assemblage a certain latitude for more flexible operation while benefiting from genetic or linguistic resources (processes of coding and decoding).[21] All of these processes are recurrent, and their variable repetition synthesizes entire populations of assemblages. Within these populations other synthetic processes, which may also be characterized as territorializations or codings but which typically involve entirely different mechanisms, generate larger-scale assemblages of which some of the members of the original population become component parts.

To conclude this chapter I would like to add some detail to the description of the synthetic aspects of assemblage theory. In particular, to speak of processes of territorialization and coding which may be instantiated by a variety of mechanisms implies that we have an adequate notion of what a mechanism is. In the case of inorganic and organic assemblages these mechanisms are largely causal, but they do not necessarily involve *linear causality*, so the first task will be to expand the notion of causality to include nonlinear mechanisms. Social assemblages, on the other hand, contain mechanisms which, in addition to causal interactions, involve *reasons and motives*. So the second task will be to show what role these subjective components play in the explanation of the working of social assemblages. The first task is crucial because the shortcomings of linear causality have often been used to justify the belief in inextricable organic unities. In other words, the postulation of a world as a seamless web of reciprocal action, or as an integrated totality of functional interdependencies, or as a block of unlimited universal interconnections, has traditionally been made in opposition to linear causality as the glue holding together a mechanical world. Hence if assemblages are to replace totalities the complex mechanisms behind the synthesis of emergent properties must be properly elucidated.

In addition to supplying an excuse for the postulation of a block universe, the formula for linear causality, 'Same cause, same effect, always', has had damaging effects on the very conception of the relations between causes and effects. In particular, the resemblance of that formula with the one for logical implication ('If C, then E necessarily') has misled many philosophers into thinking that the relation between a cause and its effect is basically that the occurrence of the former implies that of the latter. But if causality is to provide the basis for objective syntheses causal relations must be characterized as *productive*, that is, as a relation in which one event (the cause) produces another event (the effect), not just implies it.[22] The events which are productively connected by causality can be simple or atomistic events such as mechanical collisions. But causality may also connect complex entities, such as the component parts that make up a whole. In this case, while the entity itself cannot act as a cause because it is not an event, a change in its defining properties can be a cause, since changes, even simple quantitative ones, are events. For the same reason, actions performed by a complex entity can also be causes.

Linear causality is typically defined in terms of atomistic events, but once we depart from these we must consider the role that the internal organization of an entity may play in the way it is affected by an external cause. This internal organization may, for example, determine that an external cause of large intensity will produce a low-intensity effect (or no effect at all) and vice versa, that small causes may have large effects. These are cases of *nonlinear* causality, defined by thresholds below or above which external causes fail to produce an effect, that is, thresholds determining the capacities of an entity to be causally affected. In some cases, this capacity to be affected may gain the upper hand to the point that external causes become mere *triggers or catalysts* for an effect. As Bunge puts it, in this case 'extrinsic causes are efficient solely to the extent to which they take a grip on the proper nature and inner processes of things'.[23] Catalysis deeply violates linearity since it implies that different causes can lead to one and the same effect – as when a switch from one internal state to another is triggered by different stimuli – and that one and the same cause may produce very different effects depending on the part of the whole it acts upon – as when hormones stimulate growth when applied to the tips of a plant but inhibit it when applied to its roots.[24] It is important to emphasize, however, that to refer to inner processes (or to an internal organization) does not imply that nonlinear or catalytic interactions are examples of relations of interiority: inner processes are simply interactions between the component parts of an entity and do not imply that these parts are mutually constituted.

These two departures from linearity violate the first part of the formula ('same cause, same effect'), but the second part ('always') may also be challenged. Violating this second part, the part involving strict necessity, results in *statistical causality*, a form of causality that becomes important the moment we start to consider not single entities but large populations of such entities. Thus, when one says that, in a given population of smokers, 'Smoking cigarettes causes cancer', the claim cannot be that one repeated event (smoking) produces the same event (the onset of cancer) in every single case. The genetic predispositions of the members of the population must also be taken into account, and this implies that the cause will produce its effect only in a high percentage of cases. Furthermore, statistical causality does not depend on the existence of complex internal processes in the members of a population. It may also obtain without such internal organization given that, outside of laboratory conditions, no series of events ever occurs in complete isolation from other series which may *interfere* with it. Thus, even if we had a population of genetically identical humans, smoking would still not always lead to the onset of cancer, since other activities (physical exercise, for example) may play a part in counteracting its effects. The most that one can say about external causes in a population is that they *increase the probability* of the occurrence of a given effect.[25]

It is clear that assemblage theory, in which assemblages can be component parts of other assemblages (leading to the internal organization behind nonlinear and catalytic causality), and in which assemblages are always the product of recurrent processes yielding populations (involving statistical causality), can accommodate these complex forms of causal productivity. And in doing so it takes away the temptation to use seamless-web imagery. For example, the idea that there are reciprocal forms of determination between parts can be accommodated via nonlinear mechanisms involving feedback (such as the negative feedback characterizing thermostats), mechanisms that do not imply a fusion between the parts of a whole. The chance encounters between independent series of events at the source of statistical causality can also contribute to eliminate totalities and the block universe they imply. As Bunge puts it:

A further test of the falsity of the doctrine of the block universe is the existence of chance (that is, statistically determined) phenomena; most of them arise from the comparative independence of different entities, that is, out of their comparative reciprocal contingency or irrelevancy. The existence of mutually independent lines of evolution is in turn ensured by the attenuation of physical interactions with distance, as well as their finite speed of propagation – the most effective looseners of the tightness of the block universe.[26]

The two roles that components play in an assemblage, material and expressive, are related to these different forms of causality. While material components include the entire repertoire of causal interactions, expressive ones typically involve catalysis. The odours, sounds or colours that territorial animals use as expressions of their identity, for example, act only as triggers for behavioural responses in both rivals and potential mates, both of which must possess complex nervous systems to be capable of being affected this way. This is also true of genes, many of which code for enzymes that are highly effective and specific catalysts, although genes also code for proteins which play a material role, such as being building-blocks for cellular membranes. Language, on the other hand, typically plays a catalytic role which assumes that both speakers and listeners have complex internal organizations. This internal order, however, is only partially explained by material causes (such as possessing a nervous system) and implies more elaborate mechanisms. In particular, the capacity of human beings to be affected by linguistic triggers (as well as by nonlinguistic expressions of solidarity, legitimacy or prestige) demands explanations in which *reasons for acting* are involved and, in some cases, by explanations involving *motives*. Roughly, while reasons may be exemplified by traditional values or personal emotions, motives are a special kind of reason involving explicit choices and goals.[27]

As the sociologist Max Weber argued long ago, causes, reasons and motives are typically combined in the interpretation of social action, that is, action oriented towards the behaviour of others. As he writes: 'A correct causal interpretation of a concrete course of action is arrived at when the overt action and the motives have been correctly apprehended and at the same time their relation has become meaningfully comprehensible.'[28] The fact that Weber speaks of 'causal interpretations' is conveniently ignored by most students of his method of understanding (or *Verstehen*). This method by no means licenses the conclusion that all social action may be read like a text, or that all social behaviour can be treated as an enacted document.[29] The source of this mistaken assessment of Weber's method is a confusion of two different meanings of the word 'meaning': *signification and significance*, one referring to semantic content, the other to importance or relevance. That Weber had significance and not signification in mind when he wrote about 'meaningfully compre-hensible' social action is clear from the fact that he thought his method worked best when applied to cases involving *matching means to an end,* that is, social action involving choices and goals.[30] Understanding or making sense of such activities typically involves assessing the adequacy of the way in which a goal is pursued, or a problem solved, or the relevance or importance of a given step in the sequence. Some of these will be assessments of causal relevance when the sequence of actions involves interacting with material objects, as in the activities of black-smiths, carpenters or cooks. But even when it is not a matter of interacting with the material world, judgements about goal-oriented linguistic performance will typically be about the adequacy of a line of argument or the relevance of a piece of information, and not about semantics. Means-to-ends matching is an example of social action that demands motives as part of its explanation.

What about the case of social action involving reasons? Some examples of this type of social action may not involve semantic interpretation at all. These are the cases in which the weight of tradition or the intensity of the feelings may be such that the social activities involved may lie 'very close to the borderline of what can justifiably be called meaningfully oriented action, and indeed often on the other side'.[31] (The other side being social action explained in purely causal terms, as in reactions triggered by habitual or affective stimuli.) But there are other cases of explanation by reasons that do not reduce to causal ones and do not involve any deliberate choices by social actors. In these cases, making sense of social behaviour involves giving reasons such as the *belief* in the existence of a legitimate order, or the *desire* to live up to the expectations associated with that order. Beliefs and desires may be treated as attitudes towards the meaning of declarative sentences (that is, towards propositions), and to this extent they do involve reference to semantics. Propositional attitudes are also involved in social action explained by motives, of course, such as the belief in the causal adequacy of some means or the desirability of the goals. But in the case of traditional reasons for action, causal adequacy may not be a motivating factor, and the desirability of a course of action may not depend on specific goals.[32] It is only in this case that the relations between the propositions themselves, such as the relations between the propositions that make up a religious doctrine, become crucial to make sense of social activities. And yet even this case will demand a mixture of semantic interpretation of the sacred texts involved and of assessments of the relative importance of different portions of these texts for the explanation of concrete courses of action.

Weber's method gives us a way to approach the question of mechanisms in social assemblages: mechanisms which will always involve complex mixtures of causes, reasons and motives.[33] Not acknowledging the hybrid nature of social mechanisms can be a source of misunderstanding and mystification in social science. For example, social activities in which means are successfully matched to ends are traditionally labelled 'rational'. But this label obscures the fact that these activities involve problem-solving skills of different kinds (not a single mental faculty like 'rationality') and that explaining the successful solution of practical problems will involve consideration of relevant causal events, such as physical interactions with the means to achieve a goal, not just calculations in an actor's head. Similarly, when giving traditional routines as explanations one may reduce these to ritual and ceremony (and label these 'irrational'), but this obscures the fact that many inherited routines are in fact problem-solving procedures which have been slowly refined by successive generations. These practical routines may be overlaid by ritual symbolism, while at the same time being capable of leading to successful causal interactions with material entities, such as domesticated plants and soil.

In addition to preserving the objective and subjective components, social mechanisms must include the full variety of causal interactions, that is, they must take into account that the thresholds characterizing nonlinear causality may vary from one actor to another (so that the same external cause may affect one but not the other) and that causal regularities in the behaviour of individual actors are, as Weber himself argued, only probabilistic.[34] Statistical causality is even more important when we consider populations of actors. Thus, in the case of explanation by motives, we may acknowledge that individual actors are capable of making intentional choices, and that in some cases such intentional action leads to the creation of social institutions (such as the written constitutions of some modern nation-states), while at the same time insist that the synthesis of larger social assemblages is many times achieved as the *collective unintended consequence* of intentional action, that is, as a kind of statistical result. In the case of explanations by reasons, on the other hand, the collective aspect may already be taken into account if the beliefs and desires involved are the effect of socialization by families or schools. But this socialization must, in addition, be conceived in probabilistic terms. Much as the effects of genes on the bodily characteristics of plants and animals are a matter of probabilities (not linear causal determinism) and that, therefore, in describing populations we are interested in the statistical distribution of the variation in these bodily properties, so the effects of socialization should always be pictured as variable and the proper object of study should be how this variation is distributed in a given population.

This concludes the introduction of assemblage theory. The next chapter will add the only component which I left out here (the topological diagram of an assemblage) after which the ontological status of assemblages will be properly elucidated. It will also expand the discussion of the part-to-whole relation that figures so prominently in the distinction between assemblages and totalities, and show in more detail how assemblage theory can help to frame the problem of the relationships between the micro- and the macro-levels of social phenomena. Once the problem has been correctly posed the other chapters will attempt to flesh out a solution.

2
Assemblages against Essences

Essentialism is the main reason offered by many social scientists to justify their rejection of realism. Postulating social entities with an enduring and mind-independent identity, these critics would argue, implies the existence of essences defining that identity. But what exactly are these essences supposed to be? While very few realists today would feel ontologically committed to assert the existence of eternal archetypes, there are subtler forms of essentialism in which essences are introduced when taxonomists *reify* the general categories produced by their classifications. It is therefore important to begin this chapter by explaining how assemblage theory does not presuppose the existence of reified generalities.

Taxonomic essentialism, as opposed to its Platonic variety, may be traced back to the work of the great philosopher Aristotle, who created a method for the classification of entities into a three-level hierarchy: the genus, the species and the individual. For example, if the genus in question is 'animal', the method demands that we find specific differences which divide this genus into lower classes: for example, 'two-footed' and 'four-footed' animals. This new level, in turn, can be divided into even lower classes by differences of differences. But here one must be careful, since as Aristotle says, 'it is not proper to say that an animal which has the support of feet, one sort we find with wings and another without them, if one is to express oneself correctly ... But it is correct to say so if one kind has cloven, and another has feet that are not cloven; for these are differences of foot ...'[1] This method, when properly followed, leads us to the point where we cannot find any further differences and reach the level of a species: human or horse. These species may be further divided, of course, since we can divide humans into those which are black or white, musical or not musical, just or unjust, but these are not *necessary differences*, but mere accidental combinations defining individuals with proper names.[2] Thus, it is at the level of species, or at the level of what modern philosophers call 'natural kinds', that we find the essence or very nature of entities.[3]

In evolutionary theory, of course, this line of argument would be rejected. The properties differentiating one animal species from another, to stick to Aristotle's example, would be considered every bit as contingent as those marking the differences between organisms. The properties of species are the result of evolutionary processes that just as they occurred could have not occurred. The enduring identity of a given species is accounted for in terms of the different forms of natural selection (predators, parasites, climate) that steer the accumulation of genetic materials in the direction of greater adaptability, as well as the process through which a reproductive community becomes separated into two progressively divergent communities until they cannot mate with one another. While the first process yields the differentiating properties of a species, the second one, called 'reproductive isolation', makes those properties more or less durable by closing its gene pool to external genetic flows. This isolation need not result in perfectly impermeable barriers. Many plant species, for example, maintain their ability to exchange genes with other plant species, so their identity is fuzzy in the long-run. But even the defining boundaries of fully reproductively isolated animals like ourselves may be breached through the use of biotechnology, for example, or through the action of retroviruses, a fact that confirms the contingent nature of the boundaries.

In addition to sharing the contingency of their enduring properties, organisms and species are also alike in that both are born and die: reproductive isolation marks the threshold of speciation, that is, the historical birth of a new species, and extinction defines its equally historical death. What this implies is that a biological species is an *individual entity*, as unique and singular as the organisms that compose it, but larger in spatiotemporal scale. In other words, individual organisms are the component parts of a larger individual whole, not the particular members of a general category or natural kind.[4] The same point applies to any other natural kind. For example, chemical species, as classified in the periodic table of the elements, may be reified by a commitment to the existence of hydrogen, oxygen or carbon in general. But it is possible to acknowledge the objectivity of the table while refusing to reify its natural kinds. Atoms of a given species would be considered individual entities produced by recurrent processes (processes of nucleosynthesis) taking place within individual stars. Even though, unlike organisms, these atoms display much less variation, the fact that they were born in a concrete process gives each of them a history. This implies that there is no need to be ontologically committed to the existence of 'hydrogen in general' but only to the objective reality of large populations of hydrogen atoms.

The lesson from these two examples is that taxonomic essentialism relies on a very specific approach to yield its reified generalities: it starts with finished products (different chemical or biological species), discovers through logical analysis the enduring properties that characterize those products, and then makes these sets of properties into a defining essence (or a set of necessary and sufficient conditions to belong to a natural kind). To avoid reification we must instead focus on the historical processes that produce those products, with the term 'historical' referring to cosmological and evolutionary history in addition to human history. Assemblage theory, as outlined in the previous chapter, avoids taxonomic essentialism through this manœuvre. The identity of any assemblage at any level of scale is always the product of a process (territorialization and, in some cases, coding) and it is always precarious, since other processes (deterritorialization and decoding) can destabilize it. For this reason, the ontological status of assemblages, large or small, is always that of unique, singular individuals. In other words, unlike taxonomic essentialism in which genus, species and individual are separate ontological categories, the ontology of assemblages is flat since it contains nothing but differently scaled *individual singularities* (or *hacceities*). As far as social ontology is concerned, this implies that persons are not the only individual entities involved in social processes, but also individual communities, individual organizations, individual cities and individual nation-states.

Natural kinds, on the other hand, are not the only source of essentialist myths. Aristotle begins his analysis at a level above that of natural kinds, with the genus 'animal', and via *logical differentiation* reaches the level of species ('horse', 'human'). The question is, if his species can be replaced by individual singularities, can the same be done to his genera? The answer is that the highest levels of biological classifications, that of kingdom (the level that includes plants and animals) or even phyla – including the phylum 'chordata' to which humans as vertebrate animals belong – need a different treatment. A phylum may be considered an abstract body-plan common to all vertebrates and, as such, it cannot be specified using metric notions such as lengths, area or volumes, since each realization of the body-plan will exhibit a completely different set of metric relations. Therefore only non-metric or topological notions, such as the overall connectivity of the different parts of the body, can be used to specify it. To put this differently, a body-plan defines a space of possibilities (the space of all possible vertebrate designs, for example) and this space has a topological structure. The notion of the structure of a space of possibilities is crucial in assemblage theory given that, unlike properties, the capacities of an assemblage are not given, that is, they are merely possible when not exercised. But the set of possible capacities of an assemblage is not amorphous, however open-ended it may be, since different assemblages exhibit different sets of capacities.

The formal study of these possibility spaces is more advanced in physics and chemistry, where they are referred to as 'phase spaces'. Their structure is given by topological invariants called 'attractors', as well as by the dimensions of the space, dimensions that represent the 'degrees of freedom', or relevant ways of changing, of concrete physical or chemical dynamical systems.[5] Classical physics, for example, discovered that the possibilities open to the evolution of many mechanical, optical and gravitational phenomena were highly constrained, favouring those outcomes that minimize the difference between potential and kinetic energy. In other words, the dynamics of a large variety of classical systems were attracted to a minimum point in the possibility space, an attractor defining their long-term tendencies. In the biological and social sciences, on the other hand, we do not yet have the appropriate formal tools to investigate the structure of their much more complex possibility spaces. But we may venture the hypothesis that they will also be defined as phase spaces with a much more complex distribution of topological invariants (attractors). We may refer to these topological invariants as *universal singularities* because they are singular or special topological features that are shared by many different systems. It is distributions of these universal singularities that would replace Aristotle's genera, while individual singularities replace his species. Moreover, the link from one to another would not be a process of logical differentiation, but one of *historical differentiation*, that is, a process involving the divergent evolution of all the different vertebrate species that realize the abstract body-plan.

The taxonomic categories bridging the level of phyla to that of species would represent the successive points of divergence that historically differentiated the body-plan.

In addition to the roles and processes described in the previous chapter assemblages are characterized by what Deleuze refers to as a *diagram*, a set of universal singularities that would be the equivalent of body-plan, or more precisely, that would structure the space of possibilities associated with the assemblage.[6] Thus, while persons, communities, organizations, cities and nation-states are all individual singularities, each of these entities would also be associated with a space of possibilities characterized by its dimensions, representing its degrees of freedom, and by a set of universal singularities. In other words, each of these social assemblages would possess its own diagram.[7] In the previous chapter I showed how a reified generality like 'the market' could be replaced by a concrete historical entity such as a national market: an entity emerging from the unification of several provincial markets, each of which in turn is born from the stitching together of several regional markets, in turn the result of the historical union of many local market-places. Each of these differently scaled economic units must be regarded as an individual singularity bearing a relation of part-to-whole to the immediately larger one, much as organisms are related to species. What would be a social example of a diagram and its universal singularities?

Max Weber introduced a classification for social entities in terms of what he called *ideal types*. In his analysis of hierarchical organizations, for example, he found that there are three different ways in which their authority may gain legitimacy: by reference to a sacred tradition or custom (as in organized religion); by complying with rational–legal procedures (as in bureaucracies); or by the sheer presence of a charismatic leader (as in small religious sects).[8] I will use this classification in another chapter and add more detail to the description of the three types. At this point, however, it is important to clarify their ontological status because the term 'ideal type' seems to suggest essences. But we can eliminate these essences by introducing the diagram of an authority structure. In this space of possibilities there would be three universal singularities defining 'extreme forms' that authority structures can take. The dimensions of the space, that is, the degrees of freedom of an authority structure, would include the degree to which an office or position in a hierarchy is clearly separated from the incumbent – rational–legal forms have the most separation, followed by the traditional and charismatic forms – and the degree to which the activities of the organization are routinized – the charismatic form would have the least degree of routinization, while the other two would be highly routinized.

In short, individual and universal singularities, each in its own way, allow the assemblage approach to operate without essences. They also define the proper use of analytical techniques in this approach. While in taxonomic essentialism the role of analysis is purely logical, decomposing a genus into its component species by the successive discovery of necessary differences, for example, in assemblage theory analysis must go beyond logic and involve *causal interventions in reality*, such as lesions made to an organ within an organism, or the poisoning of enzymes within a cell, followed by observations of the effect on the whole's behaviour. These interventions are needed because the causal interactions among parts may be nonlinear and must, therefore, be carefully disentangled, and because the entity under study may be composed of parts operating at different spatial scales and the correct scale must be located.[9] In short, analysis in assemblage theory is not conceptual but causal, concerned with the discovery of the *actual mechanisms* operating at a given spatial scale. On the other hand, the topological structure defining the diagram of an assemblage is not actual but *virtual and mechanism-independent*, capable of being realized in a variety of actual mechanisms, so it demands a different form of analysis. The mathematics of phase space is but one example of the formal resources that must be mobilized to reveal the quasi-causal constraints that structure a space of possibilities.[10] Causal and quasi-causal forms of analysis are used complementarily in assemblage theory. To return to the example of classical physics: while this field had by the eighteenth century already discovered 'least principles' (that is, a universal singularity in the form of a minimum point) this did not make the search for the causal mechanisms through which actual minimization is achieved in each separate case redundant. Both the productive causal relations as well as the quasi-causal topological constraints were part of the overall explanation of classical phenomena. This insight retains its validity when approaching the more complex cases of biology and sociology.

Despite the complementarity of causal and quasi-causal forms of analysis, in this book I will emphasize the former. Indeed, although I will try to give examples of the inner workings of concrete assemblages whenever possible, no attempt will be made to describe every causal mechanism in detail. On the other hand, it is important to define how these mechanisms should be properly conceptualized, particularly those mechanisms through which social wholes emerge from the interactions between their parts. The question of mechanisms of emergence has major consequences for social theory because it impinges directly on the problem of the *linkages between the micro and the macro*. This recalcitrant problem has resisted solution for decades because it has been consistently badly posed. Assemblage theory can help to frame the problem correctly, thus clearing the way for its eventual solution – a solution that will involve giving the details of every mechanism involved.

Posing the problem correctly involves, first of all, getting rid of the idea that social processes occur at only two levels, the micro- and the macro-levels, particularly when these levels are conceived in terms of reified generalities like 'the individual' and 'society as a whole'. The example of national markets given in the previous chapter shows that there may be more than two scales. If this is the case, then the terms 'micro' and 'macro' should not be associated with two fixed levels of scale but used to denote the concrete parts and the resulting emergent whole *at any given spatial scale*. Thus, a given provincial market would be considered 'macro' relative to its component regional markets, but 'micro' relative to the national market. The same approach could be used to eliminate 'society as a whole' by bridging the smallest scale (that of individual persons) and the largest (that of territorial states) through a variety of intermediately scaled entities. Some contemporary sociologists have, in fact, proposed to frame the question of the micro–macro link in just these terms, breaking with a long tradition of privileging one of the two sides of the equation.[11] Given that at each scale one must show that the properties of the whole emerge from the interactions between parts, this approach may be characterized as ontologically 'bottom–up'. But does such a bottom–up approach, coupled with the assumption that individual persons are the bottom-most level, commit us to the methodological individualism of microeconomics? No, and for several reasons.

First of all, methodological individualists invoke reified generalities ('the rational individual') and use them in an atomistic way: individuals making rational decisions on their own. In assemblage theory persons always exist as part of populations within which they constantly interact with one another. But more importantly, while the identity of those persons is taken for granted in microeconomics, in assemblage theory it must be shown to emerge from the interaction between *subpersonal components*. Just what these components are I will specify in the next chapter, but for now it is enough to point out that they exist and that, if need be, they may be considered the smallest social scale. In addition, assemblage theory departs from methodological individualism in that it conceives of this emergent subjectivity as an assemblage that may become complexified as persons become parts of larger assemblages: in conversations (and other social encounters) they project an image or persona; in networks they play informal roles; and in organizations they acquire formal roles; and they may become identified with these roles and personas making them part of their identity. In other words, as larger assemblages emerge from the interactions of their component parts, the identity of the parts may acquire new layers as the emergent whole reacts back and affects them.

Granting for the time being that the emergence of subjectivity can be given an appropriate account, where do we go from there? Can we use the same procedure illustrated by the example of national markets to move up from this bottom-most level? The problem with that example is that it suggests that the relation between successive spatial scales is a simple one, resembling a Russian doll or a set of Chinese boxes. But the part-to-whole relation is rarely this simple. People can become, for example, the component parts of two very different assemblages, interpersonal networks and institutional organizations. Organizations exist in a *wide range of scales*, from a nuclear family of three to a transnational corporation employing half a million people. Families tend to be component parts of community networks, while some large organizations can contain a variety of networks as their parts, such as networks of friends or co-workers. Some interpersonal networks (such as professional networks) cut across organizations; others do not form part of any organization, and yet others come into being within large organizations and then function as component parts. None of this suggests a simple Russian-doll relation.

Similar complexities arise at larger scales. Interpersonal networks may give rise to larger assemblages like the coalitions of communities that form the backbone of many social justice movements. Institutional organizations, in turn, tend to form larger assemblages such as the hierarchies of government organizations that operate at a national, provincial and local levels. We could picture the situation here as if the Russian doll had simply bifurcated into two separate lines, but that would still be misleading. A social movement, when it has grown and endured for some time, tends to give rise to one or more organizations to stabilize it and perform specialized functions, such as lobbying, in the case of special interest organizations, or collective bargaining, in the case of unions and other worker associations. That is, social movements are a hybrid of interpersonal networks and institutional organizations. And similarly for government hierarchies, which at each jurisdictional scale must form networks with nongovernmental organizations in order to be able to implement centrally decided policies.

All of these larger assemblages exist as part of populations: populations of interpersonal networks, organizations, coalitions and government hierarchies. Some members of these populations carry on their interactions within physical locales, such as neighbourhoods, cities or territorial states, while others may take a more dispersed form interacting with each other at a distance thanks to communication and transportation technologies. The physical locales themselves, being spatial entities, do tend to relate to each other in a simple way: neighbourhoods are composed of many residential, commercial, industrial and governmental buildings; cities are composed of many neighbourhoods; and territorial states are composed of many cities, as well as of rural villages and unpopulated areas. But this apparent simplicity disappears when we add to these locales the recurring social activities taking place in them. Thus, a given city will include in its component parts not only neighbourhoods but the communities and organizations inhabiting those neighbourhoods. It will also include many interpersonal networks existing in dispersed form, that is, networks not structuring well-defined, localized communities, as well as organizations without a hierarchical structure (such as market-places) and thus without a well-defined spatial jurisdiction or a homogenous internal composition.

It is possible, however, to preserve the insight that a reified generality like 'society as a whole' can be replaced by a multiscaled social reality, as long as the part-to-whole relation is correctly conceptualized to accommodate all this complexity. First of all, although a whole emerges from the interactions among its parts, once it comes into existence it can affect those parts. As the philosopher Roy Bhaskar has argued, emergent wholes 'are real because they are causal agents capable of acting back on the materials out of which they are formed'.[12] In other words, to give a complete explanation of a social process taking place at a given scale, we need to elucidate not only micro–macro mechanisms, those behind the emergence of the whole, but also the macro–micro mechanisms through which a whole provides its component parts with *constraints and resources,* placing limitations on what they can do while enabling novel performances.[13] In the networks characterizing tightly knit communities, for example, a variety of resources become available to their members, from physical protection and help to emotional support and advice. But the same density of connections can also constrain members. News about broken promises, unpaid bets and other not-honoured commitments travels fast in those networks: a property that allows them to act as enforcement mechanisms for local norms. Similarly, many hierarchical organizations have access to large reservoirs of resources, which can be available to persons occupying certain formal positions in its authority structure. But the regulations defining the rights and obligations of these formal positions act as constraints on the behaviour of the incumbents. Because the capacities of a whole to constrain and enable may go unexercised, it would be more accurate to say that they afford their component parts *opportunities and risks*, such as the opportunity to use a resource (an opportunity that may be missed) or the risk of violating a limit (a risk that may never be taken).

Do these conclusions still hold when we deal with assemblages that do not have a well-defined identity, that is that do not possess either clear boundaries or a homogenous composition, such as low-density, dispersed interpersonal networks, or organizations in which decision-making is not centralized? The answer is that they do, but there are some important differences. In particular, these more or less deterritorialized assemblages, to use the previously introduced terminology, can still provide their components with resources, although they have a diminished capacity to constrain them. In a dense network in which everybody knows everybody else and people interact in a variety of roles, the information that circulates tends to be well known to all participants. It follows that a novel piece of news will probably come not from one of its component members but from someone outside the network, that is, from someone connected to members of the network through a weak link. This is the basis of the famous argument about the *strength of weak links*.[14] Low-density networks, with more numerous weak links, are for this reason capable of providing their component members with novel information about fleeting opportunities. On the other hand, dispersed networks are less capable of supplying other resources (e.g. trust in a crisis) that define the strength of strong links.[15] They are also less capable of providing constraints, such as enforcement of local norms. The resulting low degree of solidarity, if not compensated for in other ways, implies that as a whole, dispersed communities are harder to mobilize politically and less likely to act as causal agents in their interactions with other communities.

A similar point applies to institutional organizations in which decision-making is not centralized, such as local market-places. Prior to the advent of national markets (as well as department stores, supermarkets, and so on) market-places supplied their component parts with resources: they provided rural inhabitants with the opportunity to sell their goods and the town's residents with the opportunity to purchase them. In addition, local markets were the places where 'townspeople met, made deals, quarreled, perhaps came to blows ... All news, political or otherwise, was passed on in the market'.[16] In other words, market-places were the place where people linked weakly to one another had an opportunity to pass novel information. They also provided constraints, in the sense that the prices at which goods were traded were typically determined impersonally by demand and supply; while the decisions to buy and sell were intentional, prices emerged as a collective, unintended consequence of those intentional actions and imposed themselves on the actors.[17] But prices are a weaker constraint than formal regulations, and in any case they only constrain those buyers and sellers who do not have economic power.

In addition to the capacity of wholes to enable and limit their parts there are the causal capacities they exercise when they interact with one another. Thus, as I said above, the communities structured by networks may interact among themselves to form a political coalition, and some organizations may interact as part of larger governmental hierarchies. These larger assemblages are emergent wholes in the sense just defined: being part of a political coalition provides a community with resources, like the legitimacy derived from numerousness and unity, but it also constrains it to struggle only for those goals that the whole coalition has agreed on pursuing; local regulatory agencies participating in the implementation of a nationwide policy are provided by the central government with financial resources, while at the same time being legally constrained to operate in a subordinate position. It may be objected, however, that these alliances and subordinations are not the effect of these larger assemblages, but of the activities of the people that compose them: the alliances are created by individual activists acting as representatives of their communities, and the authority of a government agency with national jurisdiction over another with local jurisdiction is always exercised by individual officials. But it is possible to accept that assemblages of people must interact by means of the activity of people and at the same time argue that these larger entities do have their own causal capacities. The device that allows such a compromise is the concept of *redundant causality*.

In the explanation of a concrete social process it may not be immediately clear whether the causal actors are the micro-components or the macro-whole. The ambiguity can be eliminated if there are *many equivalent explanations* of the process in question at the micro-level, for example, if a coalition between communities which was in fact created by the negotiations between a specific group of activists could have been created by negotiations among other alternative activists. In other words, we may be justified in explaining the emerging coalition as the result of the interaction between entire communities if an explanation of the micro-details is unnecessary because several such micro-causes would have led to a similar outcome.[18] In the same way, a large organization may be said to be the relevant actor in the explanation of an interorganizational process if a substitution of the people occupying specific roles in its authority structure leaves the organizational policies and its daily routines intact. Such a substitution would, of course, have to respect specialties (managers replaced by other managers, accountants by accountants, engineers by engineers), but if the emergent properties and capacities of the organization remain roughly the same after such a change, then it would be redundant to explain the interorganizational outcome by reference to specific managers, accountants and engineers, when reference to many other such specialists would have left the outcome approximately invariant.

And the same point applies to larger assemblages. Cities interact causally with one another by competing for immigrants from rural regions, for natural resources such as water or agricultural land and for economic investment. Large cities, for example, can cast a 'causal shadow' over their surroundings, inhibiting the formation of new towns within their sphere of influence by depriving them of people, resources or trade opportunities. But, of course, it is not the cities as physical entities that can interact this way, but cities as locales for the activities of their inhabitants, including merchants, investors and migrants, as well as market-places and government organizations. So why not say that it is the interactions between the performers of these activities that cause one urban centre to inhibit the growth of another? Because if we replaced the merchants by other merchants, the market-places, by other market-places and so on, a very similar inhibiting effect would be achieved. On the other hand, if such a replacement led to a very different outcome that would be evidence that the phenomenon in question must be explained by mechanisms operating at a smaller scale, and that it would involve not only causes but also reasons, and even motives.

Thus social assemblages larger than individual persons have an objective existence because they can causally affect the people that are their component parts, limiting them and enabling them, and because they can causally affect other assemblages at their own scale. The fact that in order to exercise their causal capacities, internally as well as externally, these assemblages must use people as a medium of interaction does not compromise their ontological autonomy any more than the fact that people must use some of their bodily parts (their hands or their feet, for example) to interact with the material world compromises their own relative autonomy from their anatomical components. And a similar point applies at larger scales. When cities go to war, a recurring event in the age of city-states, they interact causally through their military organizations. Whether this interaction should be viewed as one between organizations or between urban centres is a question to be answered in terms of causal redundancy. If a war lasts so long, or is fought at such a large scale, that strategic decision-making at the organizational scale matters less than the exhaustion of urban resources (recruits, weapons, food supplies), then it would make sense to view the episode as one involving an interaction between urban centres, since a substitution of one set of military organizations for another would leave the outcome relatively unchanged. The military organizations could be seen as the medium through which warring cities (or territorial states) interact, much as individual officers in different branches of the military are the medium of interaction for the organizations themselves.

There are three more adjustments that need to be made to the specification of assemblage theory to make it capable of adequately accounting for a multiscaled social reality. The first is a qualification of the very concept of emergence. I said above that one strategy to avoid reifying general categories was to focus on the process of production instead of the list of properties characterizing the finished product. This is, in fact, correct, but it runs the risk of placing too much emphasis on the historical birth of a particular assemblage, that is, on the processes behind the *original emergence* of its identity, at the expense of those processes which must maintain this identity between its birth and its death: no organization would be able to keep its identity without the ongoing interactions among its administrative staff and its employees; no city could keep its identity without ongoing exchanges among its political, economic and religious organizations; and no nation-state would survive without constant interactions between its capital city and its other urban centres. In technical terminology this can be expressed by saying that territorializing processes are needed not only historically to produce the identity of assemblages at each spatial scale but also to maintain it in the presence of destabilizing processes of deterritorialization.

A second qualification is related to the first. I argued in the previous chapter that assemblages are always produced by processes that are recurrent and that this implies that they always exist in populations. Given a population of assemblages at any one scale, other processes can then generate larger-scale assemblages using members of this population as components. This statement is correct, but only if not taken to imply an actual historical sequence. Although for the original emergence of the very first organizations a pre-existing population of persons had to be available (not, of course, in a state of nature, but already linked into interpersonal networks) most newly born organizations tend to staff themselves with people from other pre-existing organizations.[19] With very few exceptions, organizations come into being in a world already populated by other organizations. Furthermore, while some parts must pre-exist the whole, others may be generated by the maintenance processes of an already existing whole: while cities are composed of populations of interpersonal networks and organizations, it is simply not the case that these populations had to be there prior to the emergence of a city. In fact, most networks and organizations come into being as parts of already existing cities.

The third qualification relates to the question of the relevant scale at which a particular social process is to be explained. As I argued above, sometimes questions of relevance are settled through the concept of causal redundancy. But this does not imply that explanations will always involve a single spatial scale. The Napoleonic revolution in warfare – a revolution which transformed war from one conducted through relatively local battles of attrition to one based on battles of annihilation in which the entire resources of a nation were mobilized – is a good example of a process demanding a multiscaled explanation: it involved causal changes taking place at the urban and national scale (the French Revolution, which produced the first armies of motivated citizens instead of expensive mercenaries); causes and reasons at the organizational scale (the breaking-down of monolithic armies into autonomous divisions each with its own infantry, cavalry and artillery); and reasons and motives at the personal scale, since Napoleon's own strategic genius and charisma, amplified by his influential position in interpersonal networks, played a crucial catalytic role.

Let me summarize this chapter's argument so far. The ontological status of any assemblage, inorganic, organic or social, is that of a unique, singular, historically contingent, individual. Although the term 'individual' has come to refer to individual persons, in its ontological sense it cannot be limited to that scale of reality. Much as biological species are not general categories of which animal and plant organisms are members, but larger-scale individual entities of which organisms are component parts, so larger social assemblages should be given the ontological status of individual entities: individual networks and coalitions; individual organizations and governments; individual cities and nation-states. This ontological manœuvre allows us to assert that all these individual entities have an objective existence independently of our minds (or of our conceptions of them) without any commitment to essences or reified generalities. On the other hand, for the manœuvre to work, the part-to-whole relation that replaces essences must be carefully elucidated. The autonomy of wholes relative to their parts is guaranteed by the fact that they can causally affect those parts in both a limiting and an enabling way, and by the fact that they can interact with each other in a way not reducible to their parts, that is, in such a way that an explanation of the interaction that includes the details of the component parts would be redundant. Finally, the ontological status of assemblages is two-sided: as actual entities all the differently scaled social assemblages are individual singularities, but the possibilities open to them at any given time are constrained by a distribution of universal singularities, the diagram of the assemblage, which is not actual but virtual.

Given the crucial role that the part-to-whole relation plays in all this, to conclude this chapter I would like to clarify two further aspects of it. So far I have considered only questions of spatial scale, the whole being spatially larger to the extent that it is composed of many parts. But biological species, the example I used as a point of departure, also operate at longer *temporal scales*, that is, they endure much longer than their composing organisms and they change at a much slower rate. The first question is then: Is there a similar temporal aspect to the part-to-whole relation in social assemblages? Then there is the matter of special entities, in both the biological and social realms, that seem to operate in a *scale-free way*. These are the specialized lines of expression I mentioned in the first chapter, involving genetic and linguistic entities. On the one hand, genes and words, are more micro than the bodies and minds of persons. On the other, they can also affect macro-processes: genes define the human species as a whole, and words can define religions commanding belief by large portions of that species. The second question is: How do these special assemblages affect the part-to-whole relation?

The first important temporal aspect of social assemblages is the relative duration of events capable of changing them. Does it take longer to effect enduring and significant changes in organizations than in people, for example, or longer in cities than in organizations? Here we must first distinguish between changes brought about by causal interactions among social assemblages without any conscious intervention by persons (i.e. changes produced as collective unintended consequences of intentional action) from those which are the result of deliberate planning. The former case involves slow cumulative processes of the products of repeated interactions. For example, during the seventeenth and eighteenth centuries in Europe the authority structure of many organizations changed from a form based on traditional legitimacy to one based on rational–legal bureaucratic procedures. The change affected not only government bureaucracies, but also hospitals, schools and prisons. When studied in detail, however, no deliberate plan can be discerned, the change occurring through the slow replacement over two centuries of one set of daily routines by another. Although this replacement did involve decisions by individual persons – persons who may have simply imitated in one organization what was happening in another motivated by a desire for legitimacy – the details of these decisions are in most cases causally redundant to explain the outcome: an outcome better understood as the result of repeated interactions among the members of an organizational population. A similar point applies to changes in urban settlements: the interactions among towns, through trade and competition for immigrants and investment, yield results over extended periods of time in which small initial advantages accumulate, or in which self-stimulating dynamics have time to amplify initial differences.

Thus in changes not explainable by reference to strategic planning, relatively long time-scales can be expected for significant changes to take place. But what about the other case? Do planned changes at

41

organizational or urban scales reduce to the characteristic duration of individual decision-making? Enduring and important changes in this other case always involve *mobilization of internal resources*, both material resources, such as energy or money, as well as expressive ones, such as solidarity or legitimacy. I believe it is safe to say that the larger the social entity targeted for change, the larger the amount of resources that must be mobilized. Given that resources are always scarce, this implies that spatial scale does have temporal consequences, since the necessary means may not be available instantaneously and may need to be accumulated over time. In addition, resource mobilization must be performed against a variety of sources of inertia at any given scale, from tradition and precedent to the entrenched interests of those that may be affected by a particular change. This implies that the larger the spatial scale of the change, the more extensive the alliances among the people involved have to be, and the more enduring their commitment to change has to be. Let me illustrate this with two examples at different spatial scales: resource mobilization performed within an organization to change the organization itself, and resource mobilizations performed in a hierarchy of organizations to effect change at the scale of neighbourhoods or entire towns.

The first case, interorganizational change, may be illustrated by the need for organizations to keep up with rapid technological developments. Given a correct assessment by people in authority of the opportunities and risks of new technologies, can an organization change fast enough *to time internal changes to external pressures*? Or more simply, can the resources available to an organization be mobilized at will? In large, complex organizations this may not be possible. Changes in the way an organization operates are bound to affect some departments more than others, or withdraw resources from one department to endow another, and this will generate internal resistance which must be overcome through negotiation. The possibilities of success in these negotiations, in turn, will depend on the extent to which the formal roles in an authority structure overlap with the informal roles of the interpersonal networks formed by employees. If a network property (such as the centrality or popularity of a node) fails to coincide with formal authority, the result may be conflict and stalemate in the mobilization of resources.[20] This means that even in the case where the decisions to change have been made by people who can command obedience from subordinates, the very complexity of joint action implies delays in the implementation of the centrally decided plans, and thus, longer time-scales for organizational change.

The effect of time-lags produced by the need to negotiate and secure compliance with central decisions becomes more prominent at larger spatial scales, as in the case of changes at urban levels brought about by the policies of a national government. The implementation of policies decided upon by legislative, executive or judicial organizations typically involves the participation of many other organizations, such as bureaucratic agencies. These agencies can exercise discretion when converting policy objectives into actual procedures, programmes and regulations. Thus it is necessary to obtain their commitment to a given policy's objectives, and this commitment will vary in different agencies from intense concern to complete indifference. This introduces delays in the implementation process, as the necessary negotiations take place. These delays, in turn, mean that agencies not originally involved have time to realize they have jurisdiction over portions of the programme, or to assess that the policy in question will impinge on their interests. If these other agencies get involved they complicate the implementation process by adding to the number of veto-points that must be cleared. Implementation then becomes a process of continuous adjustment of the original objectives to a changing political reality, with each adjustment involving delays in the negotiation and securing of agreements. Historically, failures to meet the original objectives of a policy have often reflected 'the inability of the implementation machinery to move fast enough to capture the agreements while they lasted'.[21]

A second temporal aspect of social assemblages is their relative endurance: a question fundamental in sociology, given that one could hardly use the term 'institution' to refer to a social phenomenon which did not last longer than a human life. People are normally born in a world of previously existing institutions (both institutional norms and organizations) and die leaving behind many of those same institutions. But beyond mere longevity, we would want to know whether the processes that constantly maintain the identity of social assemblages yield a *characteristic life-span* correlated with different spatial scales. In other words, is large spatial extension correlated with long temporal duration? The answer is that there is no simple correlation. Interpersonal networks vary in duration: dispersed friendship networks do not endure longer than the persons that compose them, but tightly knit networks of neighbours living in proximity do yield communities that survive the death of their parts. The durability of institutional organizations also varies: on the low side, restaurants have an average life-span of only a few years (a fact that gives them a reputation as the 'fruit-flies' of the organizational world) but some religious, governmental and even economic organizations can last for several centuries. Cities, in turn, while also having a range of durations, have instances that have endured for millennia, and most of them tend to outlive many of the organizations they house. Finally, although some territorial states, such as large empires, have demonstrated a resilience allowing them to endure at least as long as cities, nation-states are much too young to know just how enduring they can be. Thus, in some cases spatial and temporal scales do correlate, but not in others. On the other hand, most social assemblages larger than people do tend to outlive them on average even today when rates of infant mortality have decreased and average human life expectancies increased.

In the case of dense interpersonal networks, part of the explanation for their relatively longer life-spans is that their continuity is maintained by the overlap of successive generations of neighbours. Similarly, in the case of hierarchical organizations, changes of personnel are never total, that is, there is always an overlap between staff familiar with the daily routines and new employees. But in addition to this temporal overlap there is transmission of semantic information across generations, about the traditions and customs of a particular community, or about the formal and informal rules defining positions of authority in a particular hierarchical organization. This transmission of linguistic materials helps maintain the identity of social assemblages across time much as the flow of genetic materials helps to preserve the identity of biological assemblages. As I said in the previous chapter, these specialized media of expression must themselves be considered assemblages, inhabiting the planet not as single general entities but as populations of concrete individual entities in part-to-whole relations: populations of individual sounds, words and sentences; populations of individual nucleotides, genes and chromosomes.

On the other hand, these assemblages are special in two ways. In the first place, they are capable of *variable replication*, through a physical template mechanism in the case of genetic materials, and through enforced social obligation in the case of linguistic materials. Populations of replicators, when coupled to any filter or sorting device, are capable of guiding change over time, allowing the weight of the past to impinge on the present. When the sorting device biases this evolution towards adaptation, populations of replicators can act as a learning mechanism, a means to track changes in an environment through their own internal changes. In the second place, these specialized assemblages are capable of operating at *multiple spatial scales simultaneously*: genes are active within cells, govern the functioning of organs, influence the behaviour of entire organisms, and obstacles to their flow define the reproductive isolation of a species; language shapes the most intimate beliefs of persons, the public content of conversations, the oral traditions of small communities, and the written constitutions of large organizations and entire governments.[22] Thanks to the flow of linguistic replicators, assemblages operating at different spatial scales may also replicate, as when an organization opens a new branch in a different locality and sends part of its staff to transmit the daily routines defining its activities to the new employees. But the flow of linguistic replicators need not always be 'vertical' from one generation to another of the same community, or from one organization to a new branch. As with poorly reproductively isolated micro-organisms, this flow may be 'horizontal', introducing alien routines, procedures or rituals which alter, rather than preserve, the identity of social assemblages.

These characteristics make genetic and linguistic assemblages not ordinary assemblages. But however special, they should never be considered as any more than component parts entering into relations of exteriority with other component parts. When these relations are conceived as interiority relations, constitutive of the very identity of the related parts, both genes and words degenerate into essences. In the case of language this manœuvre is embodied in the thesis of the *linguisticality of experience*, that is, the idea that an otherwise undifferentiated phenomenological field is cut up into discrete entities by the meanings of general terms. Since in many cases the meaning of general categories is highly stereotyped (particularly when they are categories applying to groups of people, as in gender or race categories) the thesis of the linguisticality of experience implies that perception is socially constructed.[23] At the start of this chapter I argued that general categories do not refer to anything in the real world and that to believe they do (i.e. to reify them) leads directly to essentialism. Social constructivism is supposed to be an antidote to this, in the sense that by showing that general categories are mere stereotypes it blocks the move towards their reification. But by coupling the idea that perception is intrinsically linguistic with the ontological assumption that only the contents of experience really exist, this position leads directly to a form of *social essentialism*. In the following chapters, as I perform a detailed analysis of social assemblages at progressively larger spatial scales, these dangers must be kept in mind, particularly at the outset as I attempt to explain how individual persons emerge from the interaction of subpersonal components, only some of which will turn out to be linguistic.

3
Persons and Networks

Although persons are not the smallest analytical unit that social science can study – actions by persons such as individual economic transactions can be used as units of analysis – they are the smallest-scale social assemblage considered here. It is true that persons emerge from the interaction of subpersonal components, and that some of these components may justifiably be called the smallest social entities. Nothing very important depends on settling this question. All we need is a point of departure for a bottom–up ontological model, and the personal scale will provide a convenient one. On the other hand, it must be stated at the outset that the goal cannot be to settle all the philosophical questions regarding subjectivity or consciousness: questions that will probably continue to puzzle philosophers for a long time to come. All that is needed is a plausible model of the subject which meets the constraints of assemblage theory, that is, a model in which the subject emerges as relations of exteriority are established among the contents of experience. A good candidate for such a model, as Deleuze himself argued long ago, can be found in the philosophical school known as empiricism.

The empiricist tradition is mostly remembered for its epistemological claims, in particular, the claim that all knowledge, including verbal knowledge, can ultimately be reduced to sense impressions. Or what amounts to the same thing, that sense experience is the foundation of all knowledge. But Deleuze discovered in the work of David Hume something much more interesting than such a dated foundational epistemology: a model of the genesis of subjectivity that can serve as an alternative to the dominant one based on the thesis of the linguisticality of experience. An empiricist model conceptualizes subjective experience first and foremost in terms of *distinct and separable* sense impressions. The ideas we derive from those impressions (ideas which may constitute the meanings of some words) are not related to them via social conventions but are direct replicas of those impressions, distinguishable from them exclusively by their *lower intensity*.[1] From the point of view of assemblage theory, it is crucial that each type of impression – not only visual, aural, olfactory and tactile but also the plurality of passions, from pride and humiliation to love and hatred – possess its own singular individuality, that is, that each of these impressions is, as Hume says, 'an original existence'.[2] This guarantees their heterogeneity and their irreducibility to one another. In addition, the singular status of impressions is what distinguishes empiricist from language-based models in which a *particular* impression is recognized as being the impression of something by mentally classifying it as belonging to a *general* category.

On the other hand, some process must give these singular impressions and ideas a certain unity, even if that implies increasing their degree of uniformity and constancy. This process, as is well known, is the association of ideas. Can it be modelled via relations of exteriority? I argued before that the action of causes on their effects provides a good instantiation of relations of exteriority. For similar reasons, *the action of formal operators on their arguments* also constitutes a good example. In the case of subjectivity certain operators acting on ideas produce associative links between them and, in the process, provide subjective experience with its overall coherence. More specifically, the habitual grouping of ideas through relations of contiguity (in space or time), their habitual comparison through relations of resemblance, and the habitual pairing of causes and effects by their perceived constant conjunction, turns a loose collection of individual ideas into a whole with emergent properties. The associative relations established between ideas by these three operators meet the criteria of exteriority because they may change without the ideas themselves changing, and the properties of the ideas are not used to explain the operations that are applied to them.[3]

These three associative operators must be conceived as common to all humanity, being, according to Hume, 'original qualities of human nature'.[4] Speaking of a shared 'human nature', of course, should not be taken to imply any commitment to essentialism, since the human species is as much a contingent historical production as any human organism. Species-wide properties, being much more long-lasting than those of organisms or persons, can indeed seem to involve a 'fixed, necessary nature' when considering events at the organismic temporal scale, but this fixity and necessity are a kind of 'optical illusion' produced by the much slower rate of change of a species' properties, or by its high degree of reproductive isolation. On the other hand, a process which accounts for the emergence of a species-wide form of subjectivity leaves out many features that characterize individual persons belonging to individual cultures. Thus, while the habitual association of causes and effects allows any human subject to match means to ends (i.e. to solve practical problems), the choice of ends depends entirely on the passions: on the habitual pursuit of those ends associated with pleasurable or positively valued passions, and the habitual avoidance of those linked with painful or negatively valued ones.[5] The subject that emerges from this double process is a *pragmatic subject* whose behaviour must be explained both by giving reasons, such as traditional values, as well as by stating personal motives. We may summarize this model of the emergence of subjectivity using Deleuze's own words:

... what transforms the mind into a subject and constitutes a subject in the mind are the principles of human nature. These principles are of two kinds: principles of association and principles of passions, which in some respects, we could present in the general form of the principle of utility. The subject is the entity which, under the influence of the principle of utility, pursues a goal or an intention; it organizes means in view of an end and, under the influence of the principles of association, establishes relations among ideas. Thus, the collection becomes a system. The collection of perceptions, when organized and bound, becomes a system.[6]

This systematic entity may be treated as an assemblage by distinguishing those components playing a material role from those playing an expressive role, and those processes that give it stability from those that destabilize it. The material role is performed by the bodily mechanisms behind the production of sense impressions, those underlying the body's dispositions towards the wide range of human passions and emotions, and those that realize neurologically the three associative operators. Although Hume himself refused to speculate on the nature of these mechanisms he did believe that the basic impressions emerge 'from the constitution of the body, from the animal spirits, or from the application of objects to the external organs'.[7] To these mechanisms we must add the energy or labour that, in the form of focused attention, is involved in the continuous production of associative links. The expressive role, on the other hand, is played both by linguistic and nonlinguistic components. The main example of the latter are the ideas derived from both sensual and passionate impressions. As I remarked before, the link between ideas and impressions is not representational, that is, not mediated by a convention or a code. *Ideas directly express impressions.* As Hume puts it, the 'idea of red, which we form in the dark, and that impression, which strikes our eyes in sunshine, differ only in degree, not in nature'.[8]

The main territorializing process providing the assemblage with a stable identity is *habitual repetition*. Habit, for Hume, is a more powerful force sustaining the association of ideas than conscious reflection, and personal identity is stable only to the extent that habitual or routine associations are constantly maintained.[9] It follows that any process which takes the subject back to the state it had prior to the creation of fixed associations between ideas (i.e. the state in which ideas are connected as in a *delirium*) can destabilize personal identity. Examples of these deterritorializing processes are not hard to find. They include madness, high fever, intoxication, sensory deprivation and even deliberate interventions aimed at disrupting daily routine, as performed, for example, on prisoners in concentration camps. These, and other processes, can cause a loss, or at least a severe destabilization, of subjective identity.[10]

Personal identity, on the other hand, may be deterritorialized not only by loss of stability but also by augmentation of capacities; here we must go beyond Hume and add to habit or routine the effects of the *acquisition of new skills*. When a young child learns to swim or to ride a bicycle, for example, a new world suddenly opens up for experience, filled with new impressions and ideas. The new skill is deterritorializing to the extent that it allows the child to break with past routine by venturing away from home in a new vehicle, or inhabiting previously forbidden spaces like the ocean. New skills, in short, increase one's capacities to affect and be affected, or to put it differently, increase one's capacities to enter into novel assemblages, the assemblage that the human body forms with a bicycle, a piece of solid ground and a gravitational field, for example. Of course, the exercise of a new skill can soon become routine unless one continues to push the learning process in new directions. In addition, while rigid habits may be enough to associate linear causes and their constant effects, they are not enough to deal with nonlinear causes that demand more adaptive, flexible skills.

Finally, there is the question of the role played by those expressive components that are linguistic. These must be introduced respecting the constraint against relations of interiority, a constraint that, as I said before, rules out a neo-Kantian constitutive role for language. Moreover, it must be kept in mind that language came relatively late in the history of the evolution of the human species. As an intelligent species we spent millennia successfully coping with environmental challenges using accumulated knowledge about cause-and-effect relations. Hume himself argues that the ability to match means to ends (i.e. the capacity for causal reasoning), is not an exclusively human ability but may be observed in other animals which use it 'for their own preservation, and the propagation of their species'.[11] So to be compatible with assemblage theory, any given account of language must be capable of explaining its first emergence on the basis of a prior nonlinguistic form of intelligence. On the other hand, when language finally emerged it augmented those prior forms of intelligent behaviour through its much greater *combinatorial productivity*. One difficulty with the associationist approach, a difficulty often pointed out by its critics, is the move from simple ideas to more complex ones. In Hume's account, for instance, the complex idea of an apple would be produced by combining simple ideas for a certain colour, shape, aroma, taste, and so on. But this combinatorial capacity pales when compared to that of language: given a dictionary with a finite number of words, a set of grammatical rules can produce an infinite number of well-formed sentences.[12] From the point of view of assemblage theory there is no problem in simply adding this combinatorial productivity of language to that of associationism, as long as the theory of grammar that accounts for it (and several existing theories do) can also pass the evolutionary test, (i.e. that the formal operators it postulates be capable of emerging from a prior nonlinguistic form of subjectivity).[13]

Assuming that we have a linguistic theory that meets all the requirements, the main effect of language at the personal scale is the shaping of *beliefs*. In the Humean account, the difference between belief and disbelief relative to a given idea is simply a question of intensity.[14] Given that ideas are low-intensity replicas of impressions, believing in them simply brings them closer to those impressions, which is why, according to Hume, '[an] idea assented to feels different from a fictitious idea'.[15] This notion of belief as feeling contrasts sharply with that of modern philosophers who stress the role of language. As I said in Chapter 1, a belief may be considered an attitude towards a proposition, that is, towards the meaning of a sentence stating (truly or falsely) matters of fact. Given that declarative sentences are an important example of the combinatorial productivity of language, and that within assemblage theory this productivity is accepted as real, we must take seriously the definition of belief as a propositional attitude. On the other hand, this does not rule out the Humean notion since we may adopt such an attitude with different degrees of intensity, and in many cases it is the intensity of a given belief, more that the corresponding proposition, that drives social action. Thus, some people may be willing to die for a cause if they believe that martyrdom will guarantee eternal rewards, but this willingness to sacrifice themselves is more closely linked to the intensity of their devotion than to the specific semantic content of the belief (say, a certain number of virgins waiting in heaven), a content which could be altered without altering the behaviour. The importance of intensity over semantic content is clearer in other propositional attitudes, such as *desires*, which may take as objects purely Humean ideas (a desire for a specific taste or sound, or a particular visual experience) although they may also be directed towards propositions, as in the case of a desire for eternal salvation.

This brief sketch of how subjectivity may be handled within assemblage theory can hardly be the last word, but it will be enough to provide us with a point of departure. The subject or person emerging from the assembly of subpersonal components (impressions, ideas, propositional attitudes, habits, skills) has the right capacities to act pragmatically, (i.e. to match means to ends) as well as socially, to select ends for a variety of habitual or customary reasons that need not involve any conscious decision. On the other hand, given that the processes that produce assemblages are always iterative (i.e. that they always yield populations), we must immediately add those aspects of subjectivity that emerge from the interactions between persons. Some of these interactions may be viewed as taking place within assemblages, albeit ones with much shorter life-spans. These ephemeral assemblages may be referred to as 'social encounters', and of the many different types of social encounters we may single out a particularly relevant one: conversations between two or more persons.

The most important research in this regard is without doubt represented by the work of the sociologist Erving Goffman who studied the way in which conversations add another layer of identity to persons: the *public image or persona* they project in their encounters with others, an image that has less to do with who they are than who they want to be. Goffman's analysis of conversations lends itself to an assemblage approach first of all for its stress on relations of exteriority. He defines his subject matter as

> the class of events which occurs during co-presence and by virtue of co-presence. The ultimate behavioral materials are the glances, gestures, positionings, and verbal statements that people continuously feed into the situation, whether intended or not. These are the *external signs of orientation and involvement* – states of mind and body not ordinarily examined with respect to their social organization.[16]

In addition, Goffman's approach emphasizes the properties of conversations that cannot be reduced to their component parts, such as that of possessing a *ritual equilibrium* which may be threatened if involvement or attention are not properly allocated. A good example of threats to ritual stability are embarrassing events, such as linguistic errors (mispronunciation or misuse of words, lack of availability of a word when needed) or breaches of etiquette (making fun of a stutterer, calling a misstatement a lie), since these incidents divert attention from the conversation itself to the norms which the participants mutually enforce. When such threats occur it is the situation itself that becomes embarrassing: while the participant who committed the error may feel humiliated, particularly if the others do not allow him or her to save face, the other participants may also feel embarrassed about the incident itself, so that the entire situation suffers and must be repaired. The degree to which repair is necessary is directly linked to the intensity of the disruption. As Goffman writes, a humiliating event places all participants in 'a state of ritual disequilibrium or disgrace, and an attempt must be made to reestablish a satisfactory ritual state for them ... The imagery of equilibrium is apt here because the length and intensity of the corrective effort is nicely adapted to the persistence and intensity of the threat.'[17]

As an assemblage, a conversation possesses components performing both material and expressive roles. The main material component is *co-presence*: human bodies correctly assembled in space, close enough to hear each other and physically oriented towards one another. Another material component is the attention and involvement needed to keep the conversation going, as well as the labour spent repairing ritual disequilibrium. While in routine conversations this labour may consist of simple habits, other occasions may demand the exercise of skills, such as tact (the capacity to prevent causing embarrassment to others) and poise (the capacity to maintain one's composure under potentially embarrassing circumstances).[18] These are the minimal components playing a material role. But technological inventions (such as telephones or computer networks) may make strict physical co-presence unnecessary, leading to the loss of some material components (spatial proximity), but adding others, the technological devices themselves as well as the infrastructure needed to link many such devices.

Although the flow of words making up the content of a conversation clearly plays an important expressive role, every participant in a conversation is also expressing claims to a certain public persona through every facial gesture, bodily posture, deployment of (or failure to deploy) poise and tact, choice of subject matter, and in many other ways. The expression of these identity claims must be done carefully, that is, performed in such a way that the image projected cannot be easily discredited by others. Any given conversation will present its participants with opportunities to express favourable information about themselves, as well as with risks to express unfavourable facts. Since this information becomes part of one's reputation, it will affect the identity claims one can afford to express in the next encounter. The variety of means through which claims to a public persona can be expressed constitute the main nonlinguistic expressive component of these assemblages.

A conversation may be said to be territorialized by behavioural processes defining its borders in space and in time. The spatial boundaries of conversations are typically well defined, partly because of the physical requirement of co-presence, partly because the participants themselves ratify each other as legitimate interactors and exclude nearby persons from intruding into the conversation. As Goffman puts it, when 'the process of reciprocal ratification occurs, the persons so ratified enter into a *state of talk* – that is, they have declared themselves officially open to one another for purposes of spoken communication and guarantee together to maintain a flow of words'.[19] Conversations also have boundaries in time, defined by conventional ways of initiating and terminating an encounter, as well as a temporal order specifying the taking of turns during the encounter.

Any event, or series of events, that destabilizes the conversation or blurs its boundaries may be considered deterritorializing. Embarrassment or humiliation are examples of the former: to the extent that claims to a publicly acceptable self circulate in conversations, any damage done to these public images is a potential threat to the integrity of the situation. Goffman discusses critical points in the intensity of humiliation, for example, after which regaining composure becomes impossible, embarrassment is communicated to all participants, and the conversation collapses.[20] Beyond this, there are events which may transform a casual conversation into a heated discussion and, if the situation is not corrected, into a fist-fight. These events are also deterritorializing. Finally, a technological invention that allows a conversation to take place at a distance affects its identity not by changing it into some other form of social encounter but by blurring its spatial boundaries, forcing participants to compensate for the lack of co-presence in a variety of other ways.

The role performed by language in these assemblages is straightforward, given that what is communicated in these exchanges are words and sentences. But, as I argued in a previous chapter, these linguistic entities have both signification and significance, and these two dimensions of meaning, one semantic the other pragmatic, should never be confused.[21] One way in which the pragmatic dimension of language can be brought up is by thinking of the consequences of saying something. As Goffman argues, with the possible exception of activities deliberately intended to kill time, all other human activities have pragmatic consequences. In many cases these consequences are relatively well known in advance, due to their very high probability of occurrence, and are not therefore problematic. But other situations are both consequential and problematic. These he calls *eventful or fateful*.[22] The term applies, of course, to many types of social encounters, some of which may have a minimal linguistic component, such as the encounter of enemy armies on a battlefield. But it may also be used to distinguish conversations in which routine and relatively insignificant words are exchanged from those in which a subject matter of great importance to the participants is being discussed, and in which the outcome of the discussion is not easy to predict in advance. From the point of view of the identity claims one can make in social encounters, eventfulness changes the distribution of opportunities and risks. In particular, only eventful situations allow participants the expressive possibility of *displaying character* (courage, integrity, sportsmanship). This is a significant opportunity because eventful encounters are relatively rare and, if the opportunity is not missed, participants can enhance their reputations in a long-lasting manner, since claims to strong character can only be challenged by the occurrence of another problematic event, not by the other participants.[23]

When conversations (and other social encounters) are repeated with the same participants, or with overlapping sets of participants, longer-lasting social entities tend to emerge: interpersonal networks. From the assemblage point of view, interpersonal networks are perhaps the social entities that are the easiest to handle, given that in network theory the emphasis is always on relations of exteriority. That is, it is *the pattern of recurring links*, as well as the properties of those links, which forms the subject of study, not the attributes of the persons occupying positions in a network. These attributes (such as gender or race) are clearly very important in the study of human interactions, but some of the emergent properties of networks tend to remain the same despite changes in those attributes. This implies that the properties of the links cannot be inferred from the properties of the persons linked. The properties of links include their *strength*, that is, the frequency of interaction among the persons occupying given positions, as well as the emotional content of the relation; their *presence or absence*, the absences indicating the existence of borders separating one network from another, or one clique from another within a given network; and their *reciprocity*, that is, the symmetry or asymmetry of the obligations entailed by the link.[24]

In addition, the overall network has properties of its own, one of the most important of which is *density*, a measure of the intensity of connectivity among indirect links.[25] Roughly, if the friends of my friends (that is, my indirect links) know the friends of your friends, and they know the friends of everybody else's friends in a given community, the network has a high density. As I argued in the previous chapter, in a high-density network information about transgressions of local norms becomes known to all members of a community, which implies that the network itself has the capacity to store local reputations and, via ostracism and other penalties, the capacity to deter potential cheaters. Another important property is a network's *stability*, a property that may be studied either in terms of the attitudes of the persons involved or in terms of some systematic interdependence between attitudes due to positions in a network. In the first case, a network is stable if the attitudes of persons towards other members of a network do not produce psychological tension, as would a situation where the friends of my friends are actually my enemies. In the second case what matters is how a property of the positions in a network, such as the property of being nearby (as defined by the number of intermediary links) has effects on the people occupying those positions, making them more likely to adopt similar attitudes towards third parties.[26] Density and stability, in turn, may endow a community with a high degree of *solidarity*. This is also an emergent property to the extent that one and the same degree of solidarity may be compatible with a variety of combinations of personal reasons and motives: some members may be motivated by the feelings of togetherness which getting involved in the affairs of the community produces in them, others by altruism, and yet others by strict calculations of reciprocity.

Components performing a material role in these assemblages include, in addition to the physical bodies of the people involved, the time and energy they must spend in maintaining relationships, two resources which are always in short supply and which limit the number of friends and contacts a person can have. The maintenance of relations involves more than just having frequent conversations. It also includes the exchange of physical aid, like taking care of other people's children, and of emotional support, such as giving advice in difficult situations. As it happens, there exists in many communities a division of labour in this regard with women tending to perform a disproportionate amount of the work involved in the maintenance of relations.[27] Components playing an expressive role include a large variety of nonlinguistic displays of solidarity and trust. Certain routine acts, such as having dinner together (whether on a daily basis or on special holidays) or going to church (and other collective rituals) serve both to express solidarity and to perform maintenance tasks.[28] Other acts, such as the sharing of adversity, as happens during a strike in a workers' community, or the demonstrated willingness to make sacrifices for the community, both express and build trust. The important point is that when it comes to express solidarity, actions speak louder than words. Expressive components also include any items capable of serving as a badge of identity. The very act of using the particular dialect of a language spoken in a given community, for example, expresses the fact that the user belongs to that community, a display of pride of membership which coexists with whatever linguistic information is communicated by words.[29]

Interpersonal networks are subject to a variety of centripetal and centrifugal forces that are the main sources of territorialization and deterritorialization. Among the former the most important is the existence of *conflict* between different communities. Conflict has the effect of exaggerating the distinction between 'us' and 'them', that is, it sharpens the boundaries between insiders and outsiders. While high density itself transforms networks into enforcement mechanisms, the presence of conflict increases the activities dedicated to policing a community's borders, not only the physical boundaries of a neighbourhood or small town, but the degree to which a community controls its members' behaviour and promotes internal homogeneity. In other words, conflict sharpens the identity of a community. This implies that solidarity cannot always be viewed as a desirable property since in the presence of conflict it results in practices of social exclusion and the placing of constraints on members' autonomy which greatly reduce their scope to be different.[30] Examples of centrifugal forces include any process that decreases a network's density, such as social mobility and secularization. Social mobility weakens links by making people less interdependent and by promoting a greater acceptance of difference through less local and more cosmopolitan attitudes. Secularization implies, among other things, the elimination of some of the rituals which, like churchgoing, are important to the maintenance of traditional solidarity. Transportation and communication technologies are other sources of deterritorialization that reduce or eliminate co-presence (i.e. they create dispersed interpersonal networks). Geographical dispersion demands that community members be more active in the maintenance of links, given that connections will tend to be wider and weaker and that readymade rituals for the expression of solidarity may not be available.[31]

There are a variety of roles that linguistic components play in these assemblages, an important example of which are the *shared stories and categories* that emerge as part of conflict between two or more communities (i.e. the narratives of 'us' versus 'them'), as well as the mostly stereotyped ethnic or racial categories used in them. As the historical sociologist Charles Tilly has argued, these stories concentrate on unified space and time settings and on actors with clear motivations and fixed attributes, and therefore do not really capture the actual causal structure of a given conflictive situation, particularly one that has lasted a long time. These narratives tend to leave out anything related to collective unintended consequences of intentional action, any process of accumulation or concentration of resources that is too slow to be detected by direct experience, as well as any social effects mediated by the physical environment.[32] But the role these stories play in the assemblage is not representing the facts but rigidifying the identities of the conflicting parties, the narratives being part of a process of *group boundary construction*. In the case of ethnic communities, for instance, the enforcement of identity stories and categories occurs chiefly at the boundary. As Tilly writes, 'You can be more or less Muslim, even to the point when other Muslims deny your Muslimness, yet at the boundary with Jews you still fall unmistakably into the Muslim category.'[33] In the terminology of assemblage theory, stories of conflict (and the categories for insiders and outsiders associated with them) serve to code and consolidate the effects of territorialization on interpersonal networks.

Speaking of conflict between communities already implies that, like all assemblages, interpersonal networks exist in populations. Interactions among members of these populations may sometimes lead to the formation of political alliances or coalitions among communities, alliances being the paradigmatic case of relations of exteriority in the social realm.[34] In some cases, alliances lead to the emergence of larger-scale entities such as *social justice movements*. In Tilly's view a social movement is composed of at least two collective actors, each comprising one or several allied communities with well-defined boundaries sharpened by conflict. One of the communities (or coalition of communities) must be attempting to correct a wrong or to gain a right of which it has been unjustly deprived; the other one is there to rival the claims of the first, that is, to defend advantages which would be threatened by its success. In other words, a movement typically breeds a countermovement, both of which should be considered component parts of the overall assemblage. In addition, the assemblage must include at least one governmental organization defined by its control over law-enforcement and military resources. The aggrieved community's goal is to achieve recognition as a valid interlocutor on the part of the governmental organization, that is, to be treated as a legitimate maker of collective claims, a goal that must be achieved against strong opposition from the countermovement. As Tilly writes:

Claim making becomes political when governments – or more generally, individuals or organizations that control concentrated means of coercion – become parties to the claims, as claimants, objects of claims, or stake holders. When leaders of two ethnic factions compete for recognition as valid interlocutors for their ethnic category, for example, the government to which interlocutors would speak inevitably figure as stake holders. Contention occurs everywhere, but contentious politics involves governments, at least as third parties.[35]

Tilly discusses how the means through which political claims are made underwent a dramatic transformation in Great Britain between 1750 and 1850. Claim-making moved away from machine-breaking, physical attacks on tax collectors, and other forms of direct action, towards the very different set of expressive displays characteristic of today's movements, including 'public meetings, demonstrations, marches, petitions, pamphlets, statements in mass media, posting or wearing of identifying signs, and deliberate adoption of distinctive slogans'.[36] The new 'repertoires of contention', as he calls them, play the main expressive role in these assemblages. During the Industrial Revolution and afterwards, an aggrieved community (or coalition of communities) had to express that it was *respectable, unified, numerous* and *committed*, in short, that it was a legitimate collective maker of claims in the eyes of both its rivals and the government.[37] Of course, the possession of these properties may be expressed linguistically. Numerousness, for example, may be expressed by publishing a statement about the quantity of supporting members, but it will be displayed more convincingly by assembling a very large crowd in a particular place in town. Respectability may also be expressed in linguistic form, but it will be displayed more dramatically if a large crowd manages to stage a peaceful and ordered demonstration. Linguistic statements about the degree of unity in a coalition are easy to make, but for the same reason unity will be expressed more forcefully by concerted action and mutual support.

The change in contention repertoires during the eighteenth and nineteenth centuries implies that some component parts switched from a material to an expressive role. But there are other material components. Given that expressing respectability, numerousness, commitment and unity simultaneously is not an easy task – having numerous members makes presenting a unified front more problematic, for example – a large investment of energy on the part of organizers to hold the movement together is required. As Tilly writes, the 'actual work of organizers consists recurrently of patching together provisional coalitions, negotiating which of the multiple agendas participants bring with them will find public voice in their collective action, suppressing risky tactics, and above all hiding backstage struggle from public view'.[38] In addition, given the fact that a government organization is always part of these assemblages, the list of components performing a material role must include the weapons, anti-riot gear and the physical control of demonstrators by police and army forces. The variety and concentration of means of coercion is an important component because the willingness and ability of government organizations to use them varies with circumstances, and this variation affords rival communities different opportunities and risks: a war may have just broken out and the government might need to recruit members of one of the communities, or, on the contrary, a war may have just ended and the exceptional government controls during wartime may have been relaxed, promoting a wave of deferred claims; the war may have been won or lost, increasing or decreasing the bargaining power of the governmental organizations and hence the chances of the collective actor's claims to be successfully heard, and so on.[39]

Questions of territorialization are directly linked to the changes in repertoires of contention. When direct expression of discontent was dominant the goals of a particular movement were more local and short-term. The switch to the new repertoire implied a move towards more strategic, long-term goals and this, in turn, involved the creation of enduring organizations to solidify gains and concentrate resources. In other words, accompanying the switch to the new expressive repertoire there was a simultaneous change in the type of collective entity that promoted those claims, from authorized communities to the *specialized association*, of which unions and other worker organizations are only one example.[40] These organizations played a key role in stabilizing the identity of a movement. But there are other processes that may change or destabilize this identity, forcing participants to invent new strategies and even to redefine their struggles. Among them are what Tilly refers to as *protest cycles*. These involve mutually stimulating dynamics (positive feedback) in which

[one collective actors's] successful claim making tends to stimulate new demands on the part of other actors. That happens because some actors recognize previously invisible opportunities, others emulate newly devised means of action, and still others find themselves threatened by the newcomers. Expansion of claim making occurs ... up to the point where rivals either establish themselves, rigidify their positions, exhaust their energies, destroy each other, or succumb to state repression called forth by those whose interests claim making

61

threatens ... Over such a cycle, early phases multiply innovations in collective action, create relatively open spaces for new collective experiments, and thus give the impression of a total break with the past. During later phases, more moderate claimants withdraw from the public arena, leaving more radical and marginal activists increasingly isolated and vulnerable. Each large cycle of this kind leaves its traces in the political system: formation of new groups, alteration of relations between citizens and public authorities, renewal of public discourse, and creation of new forms of collective action.[41]

There is, finally, the question of the effect of linguistic components on these assemblages. Tilly discusses the crucial role played by general terms designating *social categories*. Given that prior to a conflict a particular social group may have already been classified by government organizations under a religious, ethnic, racial or other category, one of the goals of social movements is to change that classification. But the reason such a change is important for the members of a given movement is not because categories directly shape perception (as social constructivists would have it) but because of the *unequal legal rights and obligations* which are attached by government organizations to a given classification, as well as the practices of exclusion, segregation and hoarding of opportunities which sort people out into ranked groups.[42] Thus, activists trying to change a given category are not negotiating over meanings, as if changing the semantic content of a word automatically meant a real change in the opportunities and risks faced by a given social group, but over access to resources (income, education, health services) and relief from constraints. In short, struggles over categories are more about their legal and economic significance than their linguistic signification.

This concludes the assemblage analysis of social justice movements. But there are other large social entities that are also composed of coalitions of networked communities, and whose identity is also shaped by conflict with other such groups as well as by their relations to government organizations: *social classes*. To speak of classes is to say that the population of networks inhabiting a particular country have differential access to a variety of resources and are unevenly exposed to a variety of constraints. In other words, the existence of social classes presupposes that there are processes taking place in populations of networks that sort them out into ranks in such a way that the persons composing those networks are born with different life opportunities and risks. To speak of ranked distributions of networks, however, is not to imply that the ranking is simple as in a 'society' neatly divided into upper, middle and lower classes. This, as Tilly argues, misrepresents the complexity of the relations of inequality between groups.[43] While the location of a network in a given hierarchical distribution of resources does create a set of shared interests for the persons composing the network, organizations are needed in many cases to focus collective attention on those common interests and give them a more coherent expression, as well as to serve as instruments of collective action when pursuing those interests in order to extract new rights from the government. These organizations, when they exist, must also be considered part of the assemblage.

The contemporary sociologist who has done the most empirical work in the study of these resource distributions is Pierre Bourdieu. In Bourdieu's view, the asymmetrical degree of access and command over resources acts as a force that differentiates a population of persons sorting them into ranked groups. Unlike older theories of social classes, Bourdieu does not limit his analysis to economic resources, and hence does not view classes solely in terms of income distributions or in terms of control over the means of production. To financial and industrial resources he adds cultural ones, such as possessing a general education or specialized technical knowledge, as well as owning the diplomas, licences and credentials needed to profit legitimately from such knowledge. This distinction corresponds, roughly, to the one between material and expressive resources in assemblage theory. In addition, Bourdieu emphasizes the relations that arise between positions in these distributions. Examples of such relations are being *above, below, or between*, that is, the relations that exist between ranked groups. They also include *proximity*, not spatial proximity but the relation that exists between two groups with similar command over economic and cultural resources wherever they happen to be located geographically. These and other relations he views as relations of exteriority.[44]

The main empirical finding that must be explained, according to Bourdieu, is the statistical correlation between, on the one hand, positions in resource distributions and, on the other, a more or less coherent life-style, a term which includes both material and expressive components: the goods and services a given group tends to own or purchase; the set of manners and bodily postures it tends to exhibit; the political and cultural stances it tends to take; and the activities it tends to engage in within a whole variety of historically differentiated fields (such as economics, politics, religion, art). In other words, what needs to be accounted for is the specific mapping between a space defined by differential control over resources and the various fields of activity, position-takings and styles. Bourdieu's explanation of the observed statistical correlations is that different sets of objective opportunities and risks condition the day-to-day practices of groups leading to the development of a durable set of *dispositions*, tendencies to behave in certain ways and to display certain aspirations. Considering that both habits and skills, two of the components of subjectivity in assemblage theory, are dispositions, most of Bourdieu's ideas would seem to be ontologically compatible with the assemblage approach. But there is a major incompatibility that arises due to his particular conceptualization of that set of dispositions, a set that he refers to as a *habitus*. Bourdieu endows this habitus with a high degree of automatism, to the extent that all differences between the motivations behind social behaviour (such as the difference between causes, reasons and motives) disappear. As he writes:

If a very close correlation is regularly observed between the scientifically constructed objective probabilities (for example, the chances of access to a particular good) and agent's subjective aspirations ('motivations' and 'needs'), this is not because agents consciously adjust their aspirations to an exact evaluation of their chances of success, like a gambler organizing his stakes on the basis of perfect information about his chances of winning. In reality, the dispositions durably inculcated by the possibilities and impossibilities, freedoms and necessities, opportunities and prohibitions inscribed in the objective conditions (which science apprehends through statistical regularities such as the probabilities objectively attached to a group or class) generate dispositions objectively compatible with these conditions and in a sense pre-adapted to their demands. The more improbable practices are therefore excluded, as unthinkable, by a kind of *immediate submission to order* that inclines agents to make a virtue out of necessity, that is, to refuse what is anyway denied and to will the inevitable.[45]

Bourdieu does not deny that, on occasion, people do make deliberate choices, or that sometimes they may engage in consciously matching means to ends. But far from constituting exceptions to the automatism of the habitus, it is the latter that determines when and where such exceptions are allowed. The habitus then becomes a master process that 'makes possible the free production of all the thoughts, perceptions, and actions inherent in the particular conditions of its production – and only those'.[46] It is not necessary to follow Bourdieu in this regard. His empirical observation that members of a particular class tend to display the same habitus may be accommodated without introducing a master process. We may agree, for example, that the class into which we are born possesses its own habits, which are regularly transmitted to new generations, and that it has access to special training to develop unique skills, a privilege that can also be handed down and preserved in a straightforward way. This would account for the relative homogeneity of a defining set of habits and skills without assuming an 'immediate submission to order'. Indeed, in the assemblage approach submission or obedience cannot be taken for granted and must always be accounted for in terms of specific enforcement mechanisms. The density of the networks structuring certain communities can be such a mechanism, as can be the more analytical enforcement practices of modern organizations to be discussed in the next chapter.

The main theoretical function of the habitus, that of mapping positions in a space of resource distributions to a space of possible life-styles, must also be modified. Bourdieu conceives of this space of positions as an abstract social space defined by two dimensions, which he calls 'economic capital' and 'cultural capital'. However, resource distributions never exist in an abstract space but are always intimately related to concrete social entities such as interpersonal networks and organizations. Not only are many resources (such as solidarity or legitimacy) emergent properties of these entities, but resources that have a different origin (natural resources like oil or coal; technological resources like machines and processed materials; cultural resources like diplomas or licences) are either controlled by organizations or produced by them. Indeed, some of the ranking or sorting processes that maintain the differential access to economic and cultural capital are *resource dependence* relations that exist not between people but between institutional organizations.

One may wonder why a theorist of the stature of Pierre Bourdieu can commit himself to the existence of such an unlikely master process like the habitus. In what worldview, we may ask, can such a move make sense? The answer is not hard to find. Bourdieu believes in the linguisticality of experience, and therefore, he believes that all that needs to be accounted for is the construction of subjective experience through linguistic categories.[47] This is something that the notion of the habitus, as a set of classificatory schemes for both perception and action, can do quite well. That such an important author can be led astray by the neo-Kantian approach emphasizes the need not only for a different theory of experience (such as the Humean model I used to start this chapter) but also for a different conception of the role of linguistic categories in social processes such as that developed by Charles Tilly.

As I said before, stories and categories play a boundary-defining role in Tilly's view, but these are real group boundaries not phenomenologically experienced borders. Tilly urges us to focus not on the linguistic label for a category but on the outcome of sorting practices in a given population, that is, on the practices of inclusion and exclusion that produce concretely bounded groups. In other words, struggles over categories are about real boundaries separating groups with differential rights and obligations, boundaries that must be enforced through a variety of nonlinguistic physical interventions, from imposed segregation on certain neighbourhoods to forced migrations or reallocations of entire communities. Enforcement of categorical boundaries may also involve a variety of subtler but nevertheless effective means of selectively including or forcibly excluding members of certain categories from formal positions in organizations. An important example of this is the matching of traditionally defined categories with those created internally by economic organizations. Thus, a set of stereotyped beliefs about an ethnic group, widely dispersed in a population, may be matched to job categories as defined by a specific commercial or industrial organization, excluding members of that group from some positions and forcing them into others.[48] This matching of external and internal categories is important because, as Tilly argues, the *durability* of the inequality between groups may be less a matter of racist, sexist or xenophobic categories than about the way in which these categories affect the very design of an organization's formal structure of roles and positions.[49]

In conclusion, we may conceptualize social classes as assemblages of interpersonal networks and institutional organizations. Both the networked communities and the organizations in which their common interests crystallize must be thought as having differential access to resources, some playing a material some an expressive role, as well as possessing a distinctive life-style composed of both material and expressive elements. A variety of practices of exclusion and inclusion perform the main territorializing work, while linguistic categories code the result of such a territorialization, consolidating the identity of a class. These identifying boundaries, however, must be seen as contingent and precarious. Social mobility, for example, can act as a deterritorializing process blurring the borders between classes, and technological innovation, by introducing novel resources, may further differentiate each class into several conflicting groups. Thus, we may accept that a population of networked communities is sorted out into social classes without having to agree that these classes form a simple hierarchy except in territorial states in which classes are relatively small and undifferentiated.

Finally, as in the case of social justice movements, not only the conflicting communities must be taken into account but also the government organizations to which they must address their claims and lobbying efforts, since it is by extracting rights from such organizations that a given position in a resource distribution may be improved. This implies not only that we have a good assemblage account of political organizations, entities possessing an authority structure irreducible to network linkages, but also an account of the larger assemblages, like a federal government, that political organizations may form. Thus our ontological analysis must continue upwards to reach these larger scales without introducing any illegitimate entities. This is the task to be undertaken in the following chapter.

4
Organizations and Governments

Historically, institutional organizations have adopted many different forms. Even if we narrow our temporal frame of reference and focus only on the last two or three centuries there is still a great variety of organizational forms, ranging from relatively decentralized bazaars and market-places to centralized military and governmental bureaucracies. For the purpose of analysing the ontological status of these social entities, however, it is not necessary to confront this historical variety at the outset. Our task will be greatly simplified if we concentrate our analysis on those organizations involved in the *imperative coordination* of social action. But even focusing on the subset of organizations that use commands (as opposed to prices) to coordinate collective activity still leaves a very large variety of forms. We can further simplify an assemblage analysis if we concentrate on what all these organizations share in common: an authority structure. We can then separate those elements that play an expressive role, that is, those components that express the *legitimacy* of the authority, from those playing a material role, those involved in the *enforcement* of obedience, without worrying about the components that vary from one hierarchical organization to another, from factory equipment and weapons to corporate logos and military uniforms. These may be added later when making an assemblage analysis of concrete organizational forms.

Max Weber, who may be considered the founder of organization theory, distinguished three types of authority structures according to the source of their legitimacy. Imperative coordination of social activity can occur, according to his classification, in a continuum defined by three extreme forms (or three 'ideal types') and their mixtures. One extreme form is exemplified by a perfectly efficient bureaucracy, in which a complete separation of position or office from the person occupying it has been achieved.[1] In addition, the sphere of competence of the incumbent must be clearly defined by written regulations and may demand specialized technical training tested by official examinations. Finally, the positions or offices must form a hierarchical structure in which relations of subordination between positions (not persons) are clearly specified in some form of legal constitution. Weber refers to this extreme form as 'rational–legal' to capture both the constitutional and technical aspects of its order, and to indicate that obedience is owed to the impersonal order itself, that is, that legitimacy rests on both the legality and technical competence of claims to authority.[2]

A second extreme form is exemplified by religious organizations or monarchical governments in which positions of authority are justified exclusively in terms of traditional rules and ceremonies inherited from the past and assumed to be sacred. Even in the rare case where the role of past precedent is breached to allow for the introduction of a novel piece of legislation (or other organizational change) the latter is justified by reinterpreting the sacred history, not by pointing out its future functional consequences. Unlike the previous type, a full separation of position from occupant does not exist, the leader or chief enjoying a sphere of personal prerogative within which the content of legitimate commands is left open and which may become quite arbitrary. Weber refers to this extreme form as 'traditional' given that voluntary submission is not to an impersonal order but to a sacred tradition as personified by a leader.[3] Finally, Weber singles out another extreme form of imperative coordination in which neither abstract legality nor sacred precedent exist as sources of legitimacy. Routine control of collective action on either basis is specifically repudiated by an individual who is treated by followers as a leader by virtue of personal charisma. Historically, the kinds of individuals that have played this role have ranged from 'prophets, to people with a reputation for therapeutic or legal wisdom, to leaders in the hunt, and heroes of war'.[4] This organizational type displays the least degree of separation of office from incumbent, and is referred to as 'charismatic'.

Weber's classification is useful for a variety of reasons. First of all, any given population of organizations, even today, will tend to display a heterogeneous composition of authority structures approximating the extreme forms. Thus, a monarchical traditional government may coexist in one and the same territorial state with modern bureaucratic agencies and with a variety of sectarian groups led by charismatic leaders. Secondly, and more importantly, many organizations tend to be mixtures of different authority forms, that is, they will lie somewhere in the middle of the continuum rather than close to its extremes. Weber himself discusses such mixtures in contemporary organizational arrangements, like a bureaucracy commanded by an elected official who, unlike career bureaucrats appointed on the basis of their technical knowledge, may have been elected on the basis of personal charisma or traditional custom. Moreover, bureaucratic agencies whose legitimacy derives from success-fully matching means to ends also have a tendency to transform means into ends: that is, they tend to display a formalistic and ceremonial adherence to rules and procedures viewed as ends in themselves.[5]

Despite the coexistence of the three authority structures in some contemporary territorial states, on the other hand, the last 200 years have witnessed the propagation of the rational–legal form throughout the organizational populations inhabiting most modern territorial states, if not in its extreme form then at least in mixtures dominated by this form. This makes this assemblage – in which the relations of exteriority between components are exemplified by a *contractual relation* through which some persons transfer rights of control over a subset of their actions to other persons – particularly important. Moreover, it is only in this type of authority structure that organizational resources are associated with a position not with the person occupying it. This strict separation results in an assemblage with clear-cut emergent properties in which an explanation of the behaviour of the organization does not need to include a description of the personal characteristics of the leaders, or in which such a description would be causally redundant. With a full separation of office from incumbent the organization itself may be considered a goal-oriented corporate actor. As the sociologist James Coleman puts it, 'these entities, viewed from the outside, may be regarded as actors, no less than individuals are. Nevertheless, from the inside, they may be characterized as authority structures.'[6]

As assemblages, hierarchical organizations possess a variety of components playing an expressive role. Some of these are linguistic, such as beliefs in the legitimacy of authority, but many are not. In the traditional type, for example, there are many elements of rituals, like their choreography in space and time, that express legitimacy simply by conforming to past usage. In the charismatic type, it is the behaviour of the leader that expresses legitimacy, in the sense that he or she is obliged to express a strong character in one eventful situation after another. In the rational–legal type it is the very fact that procedures work in a technical sense: that is, that they regularly produce the desired outcome that expresses their legitimacy. On the other hand, given that sometimes it is not easy to evaluate whether a procedure really works, even in the most technical organizations the concept of 'rationality' may be used in a purely ceremonial way. It will all depend on the extent to which the quality of the outcomes (goods or services) of a technical process can be easily evaluated. The more complex the outputs and production processes, the more uncertain the evaluation, and the less clear the technical expression of legitimacy. In these circumstances it makes sense for organizations, when documenting and justifying their efficiency to other organizations, to stick to ceremonial 'rituals of rationality' to buffer themselves from criticism.[7] In the manufacture of mass-produced goods, for example, the technical aspect is strong and the ceremonial relatively weak, but in mental health clinics, legal agencies and schools, the evaluation of outputs may become largely ceremonial, particularly when these organizations express their legitimacy to government agencies issuing licences or permits.[8]

On the other hand, and regardless of the mixture of technical and ceremonial components, the *daily following of commands* by members of an organization is itself a direct expression of legitimacy. In other words, displays of obedience, when observed by other members, directly assert the legitimacy of authority, while acts of disobedience directly challenge it. Observed disobedience, particularly when it goes unpunished, is detrimental to the morale of a group of subordinates. In the rational–legal form, where subordinates surrender rights of control expecting collective benefits which then translate into personal reward, disobedience endangers this beneficial technical outcome. In the traditional form, where subordinates give up control on the basis of sacred precedent, disobedience challenges the validity of that precedent. Thus, punishing disobedience in order to make an example of the transgressor is necessary in all authority structures, and to this extent punishment may be said to play an expressive role. Punishment, however, is a component that plays multiple roles. If the organization in question spends time deliberating questions such as how to fit a type of punishment to a type of infraction, this meshing of categories will involve linguistic components. And then, of course, there is torture and physical confinement, two forms of punishment with a clear material aspect.

Like all social assemblages the material role in organizations is first and foremost played by human bodies. It is these bodies who are ultimately the target of punishment. But punitive causal interventions on the human body are only the most obvious form of enforcement of authority. Other enforcement techniques exist, particularly in the rational–legal form: a set of distinctive practices involved in monitoring and disciplining the subordinate members of, and the human bodies processed by, organizations. Speaking of the rational–legal form of authority, Michel Foucault discusses how the legitimacy of this form evolved as lawyers and legal scholars elaborated justifications for the contractual relations at the basis of voluntary submission, but also how these legitimating discourses had to be complemented by a nondiscursive, disciplinary component, which had quite different origins, not in judicial or legislative organizations but in military ones. Both components converged in the Napoleonic state, the foundations of which, as Foucault writes,

> were laid out not only by jurists, but also by soldiers, not only counselors of state, but also junior officers, not only the men of the courts, but also the men of the camps. The Roman reference that accompanied this formation certainly bears with it this double index: citizens and legionnaires, law and manœuvres. While jurists or philosophers were seeking in the pact a primal model for the construction or reconstruction of the social body, the soldiers and with them the technicians of discipline were elaborating procedures for the individual and collective coercion of bodies.[9]

These coercive procedures involve, first of all, a specific use of physical space and time. Human bodies must be distributed in space to avoid unruly concentrations and to facilitate monitoring. Every subordinate must be assigned a definite place, whether a fixed location at an office or a position in a production line, so that observation of compliance can be routinized. The model for this analytical use of space was the military camp where 'the geometry of the paths, the number and distribution of the tents, the orientation of their entrances, the disposition of files and ranks, were exactly defined'.[10] A similarly strict partitioning of time was performed, in which working rates were established, occupations imposed, cycles and repetitions regulated.

While the use of timetables to forbid the wasting of time may be of monastic origin, the definition of training procedures in well-defined time sequences, punctuated by tests and examinations, owes much to military efforts to increase the efficiency of armies through the imposition of obligatory rhythms or 'manœuvres'.[11]

To this strict spatial and temporal partitioning we must add *ceaseless inspection* and *permanent registration* to the list of components of the assemblage playing a material role.[12] 'Permanent registration' is the term used by Foucault to refer to the creation and storage of records of the behaviour and performance of soldiers, students, medical patients, workers and prisoners, as a means to enforce regulations. These permanent records are a relatively recent historical phenomenon, a few centuries old at most, so an important task for the historian is to locate the turning point at which the *threshold of description* (the minimum of significance which a piece of information must have to be worthy of archiving) was lowered so as to include common people and not just the sacred or secular figures of the great legitimizing narratives. As Foucault argues, from the eighteenth century on, the 'turning of real lives into writing is no longer a procedure of heroization; it functions as a procedure of objectification and subjection'.[13] The information suitable for these permanent records was, in turn, the output of a variety of new forms of examination: from the visual inspections of patients by doctors to assess their state of health, to the tests administered to students to measure the degree of their learning, to the questionnaires given to soldiers to be recruited or workers to be hired. While previously a physician's visual inspection was irregular and relatively fast, now its duration was extended and its frequency made more uniform. While before a school's tests were nothing more than contests between students, they now slowly became a systematic way of determining, assessing and comparing individual capacities. In conjunction with permanent registration, the output of examinations allowed 'the accumulation of documents, their seriation, the organization of comparative fields making it possible to classify, to form categories, to determine averages, to fix norms'.[14]

What processes stabilize and maintain the identity of these assemblages? The spatial boundaries defining the limits of an authority structure are directly linked to its *jurisdiction*. In some cases, this jurisdiction ends at the walls of the physical building housing an organization, but in other cases they will extend well beyond them and coincide with the geographical boundaries of an entire city, a province or even a nation. The stability of these jurisdictional boundaries will depend on their legitimacy as well on their continuous enforcement. Any process that calls into question the extent of legitimate authority, such as a clash between organizations with overlapping jurisdictions, can destabilize their boundaries, and if the conflict is not resolved, compromise their identity. Similarly, a lack of economic, military or legal resources to enforce jurisdictional claims may blur organizational identity. Another source of deterritorialization in authority structures is *crises of succession*. Weber discusses a good example of these destabilizing events when he deals with the processes that transform a small sect ruled by a charismatic leader into one of the other two organizational forms. Such sects are particularly vulnerable to succession crises after a leader's death, given the relative scarcity of charismatic qualities. The solution is to *routinize* the succession process, either by making charisma hereditary (causing the organization to become traditional) or by writing technical qualifications which a leader must meet (thus, becoming rational–legal). As Weber writes: 'Charisma is a phenomenon typical of prophetic religious movements and of expansive political movements in their early stages. But as soon as the position of authority is well established, and above all, as soon as control over large masses of people exists, it gives way to the forces of everyday routine.'[15] Routinization, therefore, is a crucial territorializing process in authority structures.

Finally, there is the question of the role of language in these assemblages. The records and written examinations that enter into enforcement practices are a good example of a linguistic component, but it must be kept in mind that the kind of writing involved here is of the *logistic* type, a very material form of writing documenting relatively simple facts – about visits and dosages in hospitals, attendance and cleanliness in schools – not the type of writing that lends itself to endless rounds of hermeneutic interpretation. It must be contrasted with other components of authority structures that play a straightforward linguistic role, such as the sacred texts or oral histories about origins which, in the traditional type, must be constantly interpreted and reinterpreted by the incumbents of certain roles, such as priests, or the written constitutions of bureaucracies which, in case of conflict of interest, must also be interpreted by specialized functionaries such as judges.

Additionally, and regardless of the form of authority, there is the role played by *group beliefs*, an emergent property of which is convergence into some kind of consensus. The coherence of group beliefs may be increased further if some specialized members of an organization (doctors, teachers, lawyers) routinely engage in arguments and discussions, and produce analyses and classifications, that transform a relatively loose set of beliefs into a more systematic entity, sometimes referred to as a 'discourse'. The systematicity of these sets of beliefs may influence not only practices of legitimization but also practices of enforcement. Thus, according to Foucault, the analytical use of space and time, the intensification of inspection, and the increased permanence and scope of records, all contributed to the development of more or less adequate technical knowledge in the case of some discourses such as clinical medicine, pedagogy and criminal law; knowledge that, in turn, increased the capacities of enforcement of those who deployed it.[16]

This completes the characterization of institutional organizations as assemblages. But, as I said above, besides an authority structure organizations also possess an external identity as enduring, goal-directed entities. As such organizations exist as part of populations of other organizations with which they interact, and in these interactions they will exercise capacities that belong to them as social actors, capacities that cannot be reduced to those of persons or interpersonal networks. The question now is, when organizations exercise their own capacities within a population of other corporate actors do larger wholes emerge? Or to put this differently, are there hierarchies and networks of organizations with properties and capacities of their own? The best example of a hierarchy of organizations is the government of a large nation-state, in which organizations may exist at the national, provincial and local levels, interacting with each other and operating within a complex set of overlapping jurisdictions. A good example of a network of organizations is a set of suppliers and distributors providing inputs and handling the output of a large industrial organization, and linked to each other through their relations to that dominant organization.

Assemblage theory should apply to these larger entities in a straightforward way, given that both hierarchies and networks tend to display similar properties at different scales. There will be, on the other hand, differences with their smaller counterparts because the implementation of strategic plans becomes more problematic, and the collective unintended consequences of intentional action becomes more prominent, at larger scales. The first question that needs to be answered when considering these larger assemblages is the kind of relations of exteriority that form between their component parts when their interactions are repeated over time. As I argued above, an organization becomes an actor to the extent that its resources (physical, technological, legal, financial) are linked to formal positions or offices, not to their incumbents. Most authors recognize the key role played by these resources but they tend to take for granted the actual *process of their acquisition*, even though this process is hardly automatic and it is often problematic for any given organization. In particular, organizations must engage in specific transactions with one another in order to solve the acquisition problem, and in so doing they may develop *relations of dependence* as these exchanges become more or less regular.

The sociologists Jeffrey Pfeffer and Gerald Salancik have developed a useful approach to resource dependencies and to the capacity that one organization may have to affect the behaviour of another when such dependencies are asymmetrical. To define these relations of exteriority, Pfeffer and Salancik begin by focusing on a given organization and a given resource and determine the relative importance of the resource. Relative importance is measured both by the *magnitude* of the resource being exchanged as well as by its *criticality*. As they write:

> The relative magnitude of an exchange as a determinant of the importance of a resource is measurable by assessing the proportion of total inputs or the proportion of total outputs accounted for by the exchange. An organization that creates only one product or service is more dependent on its customers than an organization that has a variety of outputs that are disposed of in a variety of markets. Similarly, organizations which require one primary input for their operations will be more dependent on the sources of supply for that input than organizations that use multiple inputs, each in relatively small proportions ... [The] second dimension of importance concerns the criticality of the input or output to the organization ... Criticality measures the ability of the organization to continue functioning in the absence of the resource or in the absence of the market for the output. A resource may be critical to the organization even though it comprises a small proportion of the total input. Few offices could function without electric power, even though the utility may be a relatively small component of the organization's expenditures.[17]

In addition to the relative importance of a resource there is the question of its concentration, defined by the degree of *control and substitutivity* of the resource. Control refers to the capacity of one organization to determine the allocation of a resource for another, a capacity derived from ownership rights, easier physical access to the resource, or government regulations. Substitutivity, on the contrary, refers to the extent to which a dependent organization is capable of replacing a given supplier of the resource by another. The less alternative sources there are for a given resource the more concentrated it is.[18] Resource exchanges may, of course, be symmetrical or reciprocal, in which case the organizations may become interdependent. But if the symmetry of the exchanges is broken along both the importance and concentration dimensions then the controlling organizations acquire the capacity to influence the behaviour of the dependent ones. As Pfeffer and Salancik write, 'A resource that is not important to the organization cannot create a situation of dependence, regardless of how concentrated the resource is. Also, regardless of how important the resource is, unless it is controlled by relatively few organizations, the focal organization will not be particularly dependent on any of them.'[19]

Resource dependencies exist in both organizational networks and hierarchies. While in the latter case there are, in addition, authority relations allowing an organization with nationwide jurisdiction to give orders to another operating at a more local scale, the capacity to command on a regular and predictable basis will typically depend not only on the legitimacy of authority but also on the actual control of financial resources. However, for the purpose of giving an assemblage analysis of these larger entities it will be simpler to begin with the case in which legitimate authority is absent so that the only relations of exteriority we must deal with are resource dependencies. As mentioned above, networks of industrial organizations provide a good example of this case, but it is important to distinguish here two extreme forms defining a continuum of possibilities. The two extremes may be characterized by different strategies for coping with resource dependencies.

The first coping strategy involves the elimination of dependencies by the direct absorption of organizations through vertical integration, that is, by the acquisition of organizations that either supply inputs to, or handle outputs from, the absorbing firm. This strategy yields large organizations that are relatively self-sufficient and that can use economies of scale to become dominant nodes in their networks.[20] Their dominant position allows them to control in a variety of ways those suppliers and distributors that have not been integrated.

American automakers in the 1970s, for example, were capable of keeping their subcontractors in a completely subordinate position, their facilities rigorously inspected, their quality control procedures monitored, and even the quality and depth of their management dictated to them.[21] In a particular industry a few of these large organizations may coexist as separate entities forming what is called an *oligopoly*. This separation may be strengthened by the existence of legal impediments to the sharing of information among oligopolistic rivals, at least in those countries where cartels are illegal. Nevertheless, a group of such rival organizations may become linked to one another through indirect means. Very large firms tend to have the formal authority structure referred to as a 'joint stock corporation', in which control and ownership are separated, the former in the hands of professional managers, the latter dispersed among many stockholders represented by a board of directors. Indirect links among joint stock corporations may form through the process of *interlocking directorates*: the board of directors of a given corporation (belonging, for example, to the automobile industry) may include members of organizations such as banks or insurance companies who may also belong to other boards. The overlap in board membership indirectly links these organizations and protects them against the possibility of destabilizing events such as unilaterally triggered price wars.[22]

The second coping strategy involves not avoiding but benefiting from resource interdependencies. This strategy yields networks of relatively small firms in which no organization is clearly dominant and in which the lack of economies of scale is compensated for by *economies of agglomeration*: many small firms agglomerated in the same geographical region tend to attract talented people who can find a variety of job opportunities there, producing over time an accumulation of skilled labour that, in turn, tends to expand the number of firms in the region. Thus, even though these industrial firms compete against each other they also benefit from their agglomeration and the common human resources this makes available to the entire region.[23] In addition, the absence of complete domination of subcontractors means that the relations between firms and their suppliers can involve more cooperation, in some cases forming a relation of 'consultative coordination' in which firms do not command their suppliers to deliver components that meet rigid specifications but consult with them in the very design of a component.[24] If the American automobile industry in the 1970s illustrates the first strategy, some industrial regions in Italy, such as the well-studied case of Emilia Romagna, are a perfect example of the second one. In the early 1980s the manufacturing centre of this region consisted of about 22,000 firms, of which only a small fraction employed more than 500 employees, with a large percentage of the firms engaging in the design of ceramics, textiles and machine and metalworking products.[25]

The two extreme forms to which different ways of coping with resource dependencies give rise are rarely actualized, and when they are they are only approximated for a certain amount of time. Nevertheless it is still possible to compare mixtures dominated by one or the other extreme form. In these comparisons it is important to include not only the industrial firms themselves but also a variety of other organizations, such as universities, trade associations and unions, since it is the entire assemblage that displays certain recurrent characteristics. Annalee Saxenian's study of two American industrial regions involved in the manufacture of computers, Silicon Valley in northern California and Route 128 in Boston, contrasts the properties of these assemblages. Saxenian writes:

Silicon Valley has a regional network-based industrial system that promotes collective learning and flexible adjustment among specialist producers of a complex of related technologies. The region's dense social networks and open labour markets encourage experimentation and entrepreneurship. Companies compete intensely while at the same time learning from one another about changing markets and technologies through informal communication and collaborative practices; and loosely linked team structures encourage horizontal communication among firm divisions and with outside suppliers and customers. The functional boundaries within firms are porous in a network system, as are the boundaries between firms themselves and between firms and local institutions such as trade associations and universities ... The Route 128 region, in contrast, is dominated by a small number of relatively integrated corporations. Its industrial system is based on independent firms that internalize a wide range of productive activities. Practices of secrecy and corporate loyalty govern relations between firms and their customers, suppliers, and competitors, reinforcing a regional culture that encourages stability and self-reliance. Corporate hierarchies ensure that authority remains centralized and information flows vertically. The boundaries between and within firms and between firms and local institutions thus remain far more distinct in this independent-firm system.[26]

When treated as assemblages of organizations the components of both the extreme forms as well as their mixtures play a variety of expressive and material roles. The former relate, in the first place, to the expressivity of organizational behaviour, in the sense that this behaviour may send signals about an organization's intentions to other members of the assemblage: intentions that may not be explicitly stated in the phrasing of a decision or in any policy-document derived from it. Although we may speak of 'interpretation of intentions' in this case, this will typically be *not* a matter of semantics (that is, of signification) but of assessments of strategic significance or importance. In the first extreme form, for example, an organization with a dominant position in the flow of resources can make claims on those that depend on it, demanding, for example, favourable terms of trade. But it can choose to express those demands loudly or quietly during negotiations, or to display its dominance in subtle or obvious ways. Conversely, an organization in a position of dependence expresses weakness by the very fact that it complies with demands. Acts of compliance imply an admission of limited autonomy, and this expression of weakness, in turn, may invite further demands from dominant organizations, since the latter can use the past actions of the subordinate organization as an indication of the probability of success that new claims on resources may have. In the second extreme form it is expressions of solidarity and trust that are important, since competition must be balanced with cooperation. Here what matters is the avoidance of the so-called 'tragedy of the commons', that is, the destruction of common resources due to the opportunistic actions of one organizational actor. Any action that signals a selfish disregard for communal welfare may trigger a series of such actions by others leading to the collapse of cooperation. To prevent this outcome there must be ways of making expressions of lack of solidarity part of an organization's reputation, and ways of making bad reputations have adverse economic consequences. This may involve either creating special organizations or taking advantage of the enforcement properties of dense interpersonal networks in a given region.[27]

The nonlinguistic expressivity of organizational behaviour is not of course completely unrelated to language since the actions of organizations are closely linked to processes of decision-making taking place within them. The distinction between the two extreme forms that organizational networks may take is, indeed, a distinction between modes of decision-making, more or less centralized in the case of large firms, more or less decentralized in the case of interacting small ones. But in either case, decisions will be reached on the basis of beliefs about a number of different questions, such as beliefs about possible responses of other members of an oligopoly to a strategic move, beliefs about the degree to which dependent firms will comply with demands, or beliefs about the degree of solidarity in a network. All these beliefs are attitudes towards propositions and therefore involve a linguistic component. On the other hand, when we move beyond strategic decision-making to questions of the *implementation* of strategies, particularly when such implementation involves causal interventions in reality, these beliefs must now be related to the material components of the assemblage, that is, judged by the more or less adequate causal understanding of the relations between material resources that these beliefs embody, such as the causal adequacy of a particular technology relative to the properties of the raw materials serving as its inputs. Many of the resources that generate dependencies play a material role in these assemblages, from energy sources and industrial machinery, to everything related to logistics, from storage to transportation. Labour, skilled or unskilled, is another important material component. Money too may be considered to play a material role to the extent that its circulation causes other resources to flow. As systems ecologist Howard Odum puts it: 'The flow of energy makes possible the circulation of money and the manipulation of money can control the flow of energy.'[28]

The two extreme forms exhibit different types of territorialization and deterritorialization. Networks of small firms are married to the geographical region where the organizations and the skilled workforce agglomerate. A single firm can make the decision to move elsewhere but only by giving up access to the reservoir of talent that has formed in that region over many years. In this sense, networks of interdependent firms can be said to be highly territorialized. Large, autonomous firms, on the other hand, having internalized a large number of economic functions, have for that reason acquired a certain freedom from geographical location. This mobility makes these firms highly deterritorialized even when they exist as national corporations, a deterritorialization that is greatly intensified when globalization liberates them from the constraints of a national territory. But the fact that the boundaries of large self-sufficient firms are sharper than those of small interdependent ones points to a different form of territorialization, as does the fact that in economies of scale the use of human resources tends to be very routinized and decision-making highly centralized. In economies of agglomeration, on the other hand, not only is skilled labour a crucial component, implying that the separation of planning from doing is not nearly as sharp, but it also tends to be much more mobile: the turnover rate, or the average time that a technical expert spends in a given job, tends to be two or three years in the case of networks of interdependent firms as contrasted with an entire lifetime in the case of many experts working for large corporations.[29] In this other sense, networks dominated by large independent firms are more territorialized than those linking small interdependent ones.

While the assemblages of organizations populating Silicon Valley and Route 128 realize points near different extremes of the continuum of forms they also interact with one another since many of these organizations belong to the same industry. This implies that there are, in addition, processes of territorialization and deterritorialization common to both extreme forms, those involved in the stabilization of the identity of an entire industry. The integrating and regulating activities of organizations such as *trade and industry associations* are a key component of these processes. Industry associations are instrumental in leading their members towards consensus on many normative questions which affect them collectively, particularly the setting of industry-wide technological standards. Trade associations can serve as clearing-houses for information about an industry's sales, prices and costs, allowing their members to coordinate some of their activities. They also reduce interorganizational variation by sponsoring research (the results of which are shared among members) and promoting product-definition and product-quality guidelines.[30] The degree of organizational uniformity is also increased by the creation of behavioural norms by professional and worker associations: norms that may be informal and nonenforceable but which nevertheless help to standardize occupational behaviour, expectations and wages.[31]

An important deterritorializing factor affecting both forms is a turbulent environment, such as that created by a *high rate of innovation* in products or processes. What matters here is the relation between the rate of change inside organizations, a rate affected by a variety of sources of organizational inertia, and the rates of change of technologies outside of them, in the same industry in other countries, or in different industries in the same country. When considering entire industries we are less concerned with the ability of their member organizations to adapt (given enough time all organizations can adapt) than their ability to *time internal changes to external shocks*, particularly when the external shocks become continuous.[32] To the extent that the capacity to track continuous shocks demands a collective response from an entire organizational network, the location of the network in the continuum of forms may determine the conditions of success or failure. The sharp separation of planning from doing characteristic of economies of scale limits the number of people in an organization that are involved in adapting to change, while the flatter hierarchies of smaller organizations and their use of skilled labour allows entire firms to learn from experience. In addition, the consultative coordination between firms and suppliers characteristic of economies of agglomeration may extend the benefits of learning by doing to the entire network. The faster the rate of innovation, the more a given network will benefit from the collective learning process of the small-firm extreme, and the more inadequate the self-sufficient approach of an oligopoly of large firms will become.

I have already mentioned one linguistic component of these assemblages, but an equally important one is the written contracts (and other agreements) which organizations use as a means to mitigate the effects of interdependencies. As with the making of decisions, the content of contracts will vary depending on the predictability of the consequences of organizational action: the more eventful the situation in which a contract is produced, the more labour will be involved in the anticipation of consequences. In fact, contracts differ in the extent to which their wording needs to specify all contingencies and eventualities in advance. In neo-institutional economics, for example, a distinction is made between employment contracts and sales contracts, with the latter presenting more problems of contingency anticipation than the former. Indeed, when these problems are too great (due to dependencies created by specialized machinery, for example) this branch of economics predicts that an organization will switch from sales to employment contracts by, for example, purchasing a firm with which it previously dealt with in the market.[33] In addition to the difficulty presented by necessarily incomplete contracts (given limited rationality and honesty) a decision to use one or another type of contractual form may depend on the choice of the locus of contractual interpretation and enforcement. Whereas an employment contract can be enforced internally, and conflicts over its interpretation

83

handled via arbitration, sales contracts must be enforced by courts and interpretation conflicts handled via litigation.[34]

The fact that judicial interpretation of contractual obligations may be sometimes needed implies that the population of organizations comprising a given industry must include, in addition to firms, trade organizations and unions, an entire set of governmental organizations since the very legal definition and enforcement of property rights by governments creates the environment in which industrial and commercial firms depend to carry out their transactions.[35] Unlike industrial networks dominated by a few large firms, governmental organizations form a true hierarchy with a well-defined authority structure. In some cases, industrial networks may give rise to formal authority relations with the emergence of *cartels*, but these typically fail to have the capacities of a real hierarchy. In the 1870s, for example, before cartels were outlawed in the USA, some railroad companies attempted to give their network linkages a more hierarchical form, using their annual conventions as a legislative body (issuing rules and procedures) and a central office as an executive organ implementing resolutions, but failed to create a judicial body capable of legally punishing violations of the cartel's rules.[36] In the end, what mattered in those cartels were questions of solidarity among equally dominant firms not of the legitimacy of their authority. When it comes to governmental hierarchies, on the other hand, legitimacy is not only the main expressive component of the assemblage, it is a resource which governments can use to create dependencies, by granting or denying licences or certificates to organizations or professions.

Before discussing how hierarchies of organizations can be handled in an assemblage approach I must make several disclaimers. First of all, it is impossible to discuss in the available space the large variety of forms that central governments have taken historically. I will therefore limit my discussion to those in which processes of differentiation have yielded the most complex forms, that is, those in which there is a clear division of labour among executive, legislative and judicial organizations, and in which these differentiated functions are performed simultaneously at different geographical scales: the national scale, the scale of provinces or states and the local scale of city government. If these complex cases can be successfully tackled, then simpler forms should present no problem. Second, of all the different forms that complex central governments take I will focus on the *federalist* form, since it displays this geographical hierarchical structure most clearly. Finally, to simplify the presentation, I will pick most of my examples from a single case of federalist government: the USA.

In addition to warning the reader about these simplifications, I must make four preliminary remarks. Avoiding the use of concepts like 'the state' is important not only because such reified generalities are not legitimate ontological entities but also because such notions are too monolithic, that is, they fail to capture the relations of exteriority that exist among the heterogeneous organizations forming a government hierarchy. Without an adequate notion of this heterogeneity, for example, we could make the mistake of thinking that there is no gap between the *formulation of public policy and its actual implementation*, or that a government's capacities to intervene in reality are related in a simple way to the decisions made by some elected representatives to perform such interventions. But studies of the process of implementation have shown just how difficult it is to go from a document summarizing a goal to be achieved, to the process of choosing the right agencies to carry out the policy, to maintain the commitment and flow of funds required at different stages and, in general, to ensure compliance in a long chain of national, state and local governmental organizations with overlapping jurisdictions. In many cases, central policy decisions end up either not implemented or changed beyond recognition. Joint action by many governmental organizations is thus objectively complex and problematic, not something that can be taken for granted.[37] Of course, the complex relation between policy formulation and implementation may be interpreted as implying that the two activities form a seamless web: an interpretation that would bring us back to a monolithic concept. But it can also be modelled as a nonlinear process involving feedback, a process of formulation–implementation–reformulation that does not jeopardize the 'ability to assess the extent of goal attainment and the distribution of authority between elected and appointed officials'.[38]

The second preliminary remark expands on this last point. The relations between government organizations staffed by elected officials (that is, democratic or representative organizations) and those run by non-elected, career bureaucrats are problematic in a deeper sense. In order for bureaucracies to be run efficiently, a sharp *separation between politics and administration* is necessary: that is, the expertise of a professional body of bureaucrats must be isolated from the contingencies of the electoral process. But the more this separation is achieved, the greater the sense that bureaucracies are not responsive to public concerns as expressed in electoral outcomes. In other words, the same factors that promote efficiency tend to undermine legitimacy, at least in democratic regimes. One element of this conflict is common to many social relations that involve delegation of authority. In one model (the 'principal-agent' model) the problem is framed like this: how can employers (the principals) make sure that no cheating and shirking will occur if they have less expertise than the agents they hire and to whom they delegate authority? In this model the basic conflict emerges from *expertise asymmetries*, and may be applied at larger scales because neither presidents nor legislators (nor their respective staffs) have the specialized knowledge needed to assess the performance of bureaucracies.[39] But this model leaves out other problems that do not have counterparts at smaller scales. In particular, the very expertise asymmetries that favour bureaucracies may be turned against them, since in many cases (atomic power, pharmaceutical products, financial processes) the industries that government agencies are supposed to regulate supply them with the very technical information they need to enforce regulations. In other words, regulatory agencies may become captive of special interests, that is, dependent on their technical resources, further eroding their already questionable legitimacy.[40]

The third and fourth preliminary remarks concern distinctions that are crucial within assemblage theory but that are not necessarily drawn in other approaches. First of all, we must distinguish between the hierarchy of organizations forming a federal (or other form of) government from the territorial entity such as hierarchy controls. The territorial entity includes, beside government organizations, an entire population of other organizations; populations of persons and interpersonal networks; cities, regions and provinces; and geopolitical relations of exteriority with other territorial entities. When a political revolution changes one government regime by another, an autocratic regime by a democratic one, for example, it typically leaves untouched the previous unequal relations between cities, regions and provinces, not to mention the geostrategic position of the country relative to other countries. On the other hand, this distinction should be made carefully since most hierarchies of organizations are not really separable from the territory they govern, and part of what defines their identity is exercising actual control over the borders of that territory. Unlike interpersonal networks or institutional organizations which, thanks to communications technologies, may exist without well-defined spatial boundaries (or even in virtual form on the

Internet) complex organizational hierarchies can hardly be conceptualized outside the territory they control or the resources (natural and
demographic) associated with that territory. Nevertheless, in what
follows I will emphasize the characteristics of the assemblage of
organizations itself leaving the analysis of the territorial aspects for the
next chapter.

In addition to distinguishing the hierarchical assemblage of organizations from the kingdom, empire or nation-state that it controls, it is
important to separate for the purposes of analysis the enduring assemblage
itself from its interactions with other organizations, with coalitions of
networks, or with populations of individual persons. Some of these
interactions may also yield assemblages, constituting complex political
situations: assemblages that are large-scale counterparts of conversations
among persons. In the previous chapter I discussed Charles Tilly's ideas
about social justice movements as assemblages of coalitions of networks
and government organizations acting as interlocutors. Tilly sees public
demonstrations as large-scale conversations between a movement, a
countermovement and the police. More generally, he writes that, whether
'in the ritual executions, processions, celebrations, and militia marches of
the early French Revolution or the public meetings, petition drives,
lobbying, demonstrations, and association-forming of contemporary
Western social movements, we witness the conversational combination
of incessant improvisation, innovation, and constraint'.[41]

Like personal conversations, in which claims to a public persona are
made by its participants, conversations between organizations (or
between organizations and network coalitions) also involve claim-
making and collective production of identities: the identities of an ethnic
community or of an industrial sector, for example. But like personal
conversations, these interactions are highly episodic and do not
necessarily change the identity of the government itself, except in the
case of political revolutions. Also, conversations are only one example of
a social encounter, a term that encompasses a wide variety of episodic
assemblages – a point that applies at larger scales as well. Thus, in what
follows, I will give an assemblage analysis of the hierarchical assemblage
of organizations first, and then add a single example of the large variety of
episodic assemblages it forms through its interactions.

As in all assemblages possessing a command structure, the expressive
role is played by those components involved in the legitimization of
authority, while the material role is played by components involved in its

enforcement. In the USA, for instance, there are two main sources of legitimacy at this scale, the constitution and the electoral process. The constitution is, of course, a linguistic component, a binding written document specifying, among other things, the relations between executive, legislative and judicial organizations, as well as those between organizations operating within national, state and local jurisdictions. The electoral process is a nonlinguistic component endowing elected officials with legitimacy to the extent that its outcomes express the will of the population. But the mere ceremonial conduct of elections does not, in fact, ensure that there will be proportional representation of the different groups in the electorate. There are technical features of voting procedures, such as how are votes aggregated or how winners are selected, that impinge directly on the question of how well the preferences of a population are expressed in electoral outcomes, and hence, how representative and legitimate are the results.

There are, for example, voting systems in which voters only have one vote, and in which the candidate with more votes wins (plurality voting); systems in which voters get many votes that they can allocate in different forms (approval voting); and systems in which votes determine not a yes-or-no choice but a ranking of the candidates (preference voting). The capacities of these voting systems to express actual distributions of collective preferences are quite different, as are their vulnerabilities to strategic (or tactical) voting, that is, voting not for one's real preference but to prevent someone else from winning.[42] Although mathematicians disagree on which system is best – and given that voting may be performed for many different purposes, there may not be a best choice – they all agree that plurality voting is technically the worst, so its survival in modern nations such as the USA may be explained by its ceremonial value.

If these were the only two sources of legitimacy, then the problem of bureaucracies would be insoluble and lead to continuous crises: bureaucrats are not elected officials so they cannot draw legitimacy from electoral outcomes, and the constitution is mostly silent about the status of bureaucracies and about the legitimacy of delegating to them investigative, prosecutorial and adjudicating authority: a delegation which would seem to violate the doctrine of separation of powers.[43] But there are other sources of legitimacy. When discussing Weber's theory of authority I mentioned that in the rational–legal form the technical efficiency of procedures itself is an expression of legitimacy. In

France and England, where bureaucracies emerged prior to democratic regimes and were staffed with members of an elite public service, technical efficiency often played this legitimizing role. But in the USA the opposite historical sequence occurred, so that it was only in the context of the Great Depression of the 1930s that disinterested expertise was used as a pragmatic justification for the existence of bureaucracies.[44] Even then, however, distrust of specialist knowledge (as opposed to the more generalist knowledge possessed by elected officials) made this a precarious expression. So another expression of legitimacy soon appeared: the *fairness of the procedures* used in bureaucracies, as well as the degree to which these procedures were standardized across all commissions and agencies. These questions were codified in 1946 in the Administrative Procedure Act. As with the fairness of voting procedures there are technical issues involved, so the problem is not one of negotiating the meaning of the word 'fair'. In the hearings conducted by regulatory agencies, for example, the roles of judge and prosecutor cannot be played by the same staff member without introducing bias. The Act had to, therefore, create a special group of hearing examiners isolated from such conflicts of interest, in order to increase the legitimacy of administrative justice.[45]

Much as physical punishment and confinement can be used to enforce authority on individual persons, military and police organizations can be used by central governments to secure compliance from bureaucracies and local officials. Systematic reliance on physical force, however, signals an unstable form of authority, so other material components must be added to these to align enforcement and legitimacy. Presidents and legislators have the capacity to control bureaucrats in a variety of ways: presidents have the power of appointment and removal of key personnel, as well as control of financial resources; legislators can exercise control by *designing* bureaucracies, that is, they can build incentives against cheating and shirking into the very legal mandates that establish the goals and legal form of a new agency. Careful quantitative studies based on the principal-agent model have shown that executive and legislative organizations not only have these capacities but that they actually exercise them.[46] Congress also has oversight committees that monitor bureaucratic efficiency, and the courts can perform judicial reviews to make sure that due process is respected in the conduct of administrative justice.

When considering processes of territorialization it is important to distinguish between the identity of individual policies and the identity of the assemblage of organizations itself. The relative political autonomy of bureaucracies is clearly not a stabilizing factor in the former case, but it is so in the latter. Before a merit system and a career civil service were instituted in the USA in 1883, for example, bureaucratic offices were considered spoils to be given to the winners of an election. In that 'spoils era', the identity of the entire assemblage could be affected by episodic shifts in public opinion. But once a certain degree of insulation from politics was achieved, bureaucracies became sources of continuity and long-term coherence. In a sense, since the legal mandate that brings a bureaucratic agency into existence may reflect policies different from those of currently elected officials, political insulation may provide a mechanism for policy integration across different administrations.[47] Given that the relative autonomy of bureaucracies is partly based on expertise asymmetries, a main territorializing process is the *professionalization* of civil service personnel, a professionalization that has taken different forms in different countries. In France, for example, it was closely linked to the training of civil servants in elite universities and polytechnics, a common educational basis that instilled an *ésprit de corps* on potential candidates. In England, it was through on-the-job training that expertise was passed to new recruits: a learning process that fostered loyalty to the office itself as opposed to its current incumbents.[48]

Among the deterritorializing processes that affect the identity of these assemblages from within (as opposed to from without, as in political revolutions) two stand out: coups d'état and constitutional crises. The former involves a change of regime forced on central organizations by other government organizations, typically military ones, or by organizations that have wrestled control of the army from the executive branch. A coup d'état is not only destabilizing as an event. Even when it is over the new incumbents will typically possess very little legitimacy (in the eyes of other government organizations as well as the rest of the population) and will have to resort to physical coercion as the main instrument of authority enforcement.[49] Constitutional crises can have a wide variety of causes, such as a succession crisis due to ambiguous electoral results. But a crisis may involve a more complex situation in which different government organizations are pitted against each other. Executive organizations, for example, may refuse to recognize the legitimacy of legislative ones, calling for their dissolution, while at the same time a legislative body may question the legitimacy of a president's actions and call for his impeachment. (Something like this happened in Russia in

1993.) On the other hand, the conflict may involve not two branches of government but organizations operating at different geographical scales, as when local or state governments refuse to obey central commands. In the nineteenth century, for example, the conflict over slavery in the USA proved insoluble via existing mechanisms (such as Supreme Court decisions), provoked the secession of eleven southern states, and had to be resolved by civil war, and by the constitutional amendment that eventually outlawed the practice.

There is, finally, the question of the role that linguistic components play in these assemblages. I mentioned above the variety of means that executive, legislative and judicial organizations have to control bureaucracies. Those means, however, are mostly of strategic value, being useful in securing overall compliance but powerless to determine specific outcomes, given that administrative agencies may use their relative insulation from politics to shape the implementation of centrally decided policies. Tactical means, such as the unambiguous wording of the original policy document (or statute), must also be used to maintain the integrity of policy decisions.[50] I also mentioned the most crucial binding document in many countries: the basis for more or less codified forms of *constitutional or basic law*. These laws not only consolidate the identity of the assemblage (i.e. they perform a coding operation to complement the effects of territorialization), they also limit the kinds of other laws legislative organizations may create. These other laws vary in their degree of codification and in the extent to which custom and precedent may affect their interpretation, as in the difference between the *common law* prevalent in England and its ex-colonies, and the more systematic, less precedent-bound, *civil law* prevalent in the countries of Continental Europe and their ex-colonies. These and other written laws form the institutional environment for the economic organizations that I discussed before, as well as for all the other social assemblages we have considered so far.[51]

This brings me to the question of the more or less episodic interactions between hierarchical assemblages of organizations and other social entities. Of all the different interactions I will pick a single one, interactions with a population of persons, and of all the different political situations in which these interactions may take place I will select the situation created by the existence of armed conflict, whether external or internal. On the material side, this situation calls for both recruitment of people – sometimes voluntary, sometimes coerced – as well as the necessary taxation to pay for war. The central policies in which these goals are stated (a draft resolution, a change in fiscal policy) must take into consideration resistance from the target groups, so they involve concessions and political dialogue. The situation may be framed in resource-dependence terms: taxes and military recruits are such an important resource for a government that it comes to depend on its population to obtain them, thereby becoming subject to its demands. In fact, according to Charles Tilly, this is exactly how modern rights of citizenship came into being in Europe in the seventeenth and eighteenth centuries, as governments engaged in the expansion of their armies (and of the taxes needed to pay for them) had to bargain with the target-groups and yield to their demands for political participation.[52]

On the expressive side, these situations call for a variety of means – some symbolic, some directly expressive – to strengthen the unity of a government and the population. The classical example is the effect that the French Revolution had on the composition of armies, that is, the change from mercenary to loyal citizen armies. The means used to effect this change in different countries, however, varied with the existing sources of legitimacy. Two of the forms of legitimacy discussed by Weber, traditional and rational–legal, have counterparts at larger scales. In some countries the bonds uniting a population are inherited or come from a long tradition, so that the 'nation' precedes the 'state'. In others, these bonds emerge from the sharing of the same laws, that is, the 'state' precedes the 'nation'.[53] Countries that followed the state-to-nation path (such as France or England) tended to favour newly invented expressions of patriotism: flags, oaths, anthems, national holidays, military parades, official celebrations. Those that followed the nation-to-state path (Germany) tended towards more populist expressions, using more or less coherent syntheses of popular elements created by intellectual elites. However, just as Weber's ideal types rarely exist in pure form, blood and law as sources of national unity were never mutually exclusive. Most countries used a mix of these two sources of legitimacy when rallying their populations for war. And ultimately, regardless of what combination of expressive means a given government used, the ultimate display of patriotism has always been the willingness of citizens to die for their country, as expressed behaviourally on the battlefield.

The reality or threat of armed conflict is itself a powerful territorializing force, making people rally behind their governments and close ranks with each other. Much as the solidarity binding a community may be transformed into social exclusion when conflict with other communities sharpens their sense of 'us' versus 'them', external war can transform a simple emotional attachment to a country's traditions and institutions into a sense of superiority relative to enemy countries and their allies. Loyalty, which need not involve comparisons with others, is transformed into hostility and xenophobia. Internal war, on the other hand, can act as a deterritorializing force, either by destabilizing a government through constant riots and turmoil or by drastically changing its very identity, from one regime to another, as in successful political revolutions. Unlike coups d'état, revolutions go beyond interactions between government organizations. The minimum assemblage, a recurrent one in past revolutions, includes: a population that has undergone a period of relative prosperity and rising expectations, followed by a period of deprivation when those expectations are frustrated; a struggle between dominant coalitions and those who challenge them; and displays of vulnerability by government organizations, such as a decrease in their enforcement capacities due to a fiscal crisis, a bad economy or a military defeat abroad.[54]

While for the citizens of a given country external warfare may not have a definite spatial dimension, in the sense that they may form xenophobic beliefs without a clear sense of the territorial situation of 'us' versus 'them', for government organizations this is not typically the case, unless the threat comes from terrorist organizations lacking any territorial base. For most of their modern history, however, governmental hierarchies have operated within concrete geopolitical entities, such as nation-states, kingdoms or empires. Moreover, international law, as it developed in the West after the peace treaty that ended the Thirty Years War in the seventeenth century, was intimately related to spatial questions, such as legal definitions of sovereignty within bounded spatial territories, and geostrategic questions defining the military opportunities and risks that different organizational hierarchies had to face. Thus, we have reached the limits of what can be analysed without reference to the spatial aspects of assemblages. In the following chapter I will return to the analysis of government organizations and of the processes that produced modern nation-states, once I have dealt with the spatial aspects of assemblages at smaller scales, from buildings and neighbourhoods to cities and the hierarchies and networks that urban centres form.

5
Cities and Nations

Interpersonal networks and institutional organizations may be studied without reference to their location in space because communication technologies allow their defining linkages and formal positions to be created and maintained at a distance, but as we move to larger scales spatial relations become crucial. Social entities like cities, for example, composed of entire populations of persons, networks and organizations, can hardly be conceptualized without a physical infrastructure of buildings, streets and various conduits for the circulation of matter and energy, defined in part by their spatial relations to one another. In fact, sociologists discovered the social relations generated by territoriality in the 1920s when the famous Chicago school began its studies of urban contexts, viewed both as spatial localities as well as sites structured in time by habitual or customary practices.[1] More recently sociologists such as Anthony Giddens, influenced in part by the work of urban geographers, have returned to this theme, reconceptualizing social territories through the notion of a 'regionalized locale'. As Giddens writes:

> Locales refer to the use of space to provide the *settings* of interaction, the settings of interaction in turn being essential to specifying *contextuality* ... Locales may range from a room in a house, a street corner, the shop floor of a factory, towns and cities, to the territorially demarcated areas occupied by nation-states. But locales are typically internally regionalized, and the regions within them are of critical importance in constituting contexts of interaction ... One of the

reasons for using the term 'locale' rather than place is that the properties of settings are employed in a chronic way by agents in the constitution of encounters across space and time. [Locales can be] 'stopping places' in which the physical mobility of agents' trajectories is arrested or curtailed for the duration of encounters or social occasions ... 'Regionalization' should be understood not merely as localization in space but as referring to the zoning of time-space in relation to routinized social practices. Thus a private house is a locale which is a 'station' for a large cluster of interactions in the course of a typical day. Houses in contemporary societies are regionalized into floors, halls and rooms. But the various zones of the house are zoned differently in time as well as space. The rooms downstairs are characteristically used mostly in daylight hours, while bedrooms are where individuals 'retire to' at night.[2]

Giddens' description of regionalized locales, as physical territories structured in time by social rhythms, lends itself nicely to an assemblage approach, providing his definition is augmented with the expressive elements with which locales and regions distinguish themselves from each other. The stress on rhythmic or periodic routines, however, would seem to present a problem. I have argued in previous chapters that, except in the most uneventful situations, routine behaviour must be complemented with deliberate decision-making in the explanation of social action. But when studying the effect of human behaviour on the form of urban components the emphasis on routine activity is justified because, as the historian Fernand Braudel reminds us, urban forms tend to change extremely slowly. A house, as he says, 'wherever it may be, is an enduring thing, and it bears witness to the slow pace of civilizations, of cultures bent on preserving, maintaining, repeating'.[3] Given this slowness it seems correct to emphasize those human activities that are so regular they have a chance to impinge on urban form in the long run, such as the journeys to work or journeys to shop that give cities their daily rhythms. On the other hand, in those cases where we witness historical accelerations of this slow pace we will have to add choice to routines since acceleration in the change of urban form typically implies breaks with tradition and hence, deliberate design.

Let us now give an assemblage analysis of these regionalized locales, starting with individual buildings. The material role in buildings is played, first of all, by those components that allow them to be successful *load-*

bearing structures. For buildings that are a few storeys high, the walls themselves perform this task, in conjunction with columns and independent beams, but large governmental, religious and corporate buildings must make use of more sophisticated techniques as they become taller. As skyscraper designers know well, radical changes in form may be needed once a critical height has been reached, such as the use of an interconnected iron or steel frame which, beginning in the 1850s, liberated walls from their load-bearing duties transforming them into mere curtains. Other components playing a material role are those determining the *connectivity* of the regions of a building. If locales are stations where the daily paths of individual persons converge, the regions that subdivide them must be connected to each other to allow for the circulation of human bodies and a variety of other material entities.[4] In a simple dwelling, this connectivity is effected via doors, hallways and staircases shaping the flow of people, and by windows for the circulation of air and light. In taller buildings, on the other hand, internal transportation technology may be needed. Thus, the same decade that saw the introduction of the internal metallic frame also witnessed the transformation of old mechanical lifting devices into the earliest elevators, and a corresponding transformation in the vertical connectivity of buildings.

Changes in connectivity, in turn, impinge in a variety of ways on the social activities performed in a given locale. Fernand Braudel, for example, argues that the connectivity of some residential buildings in the eighteenth century changed dramatically at the same time that the function of the rooms became more specialized, with the bedroom in particular becoming a fully detached region. As he writes, the new connectivity contrasted sharply with that which characterized previous buildings:

> In a Parisian town house of the seventeenth century, on the first floor, which was the noble storey, reserved for the owners of the house, all the rooms – antechambers, salons, galleries and bedrooms – opened off each other and were sometimes hard to tell apart. Everyone, including servants on domestic errands, had to go through all of them to reach the stairs.[5]

A hundred years later, some rooms had become public while others were strictly private, partly as a result of the fact that the routine circulation through a house was now constrained by a different distribution of doors and hallways. Privacy, in a sense, was created by the new regionalization of these locales. In nonresidential buildings the changes in connectivity brought about by elevators altered the form of the circulation of employees, from a horizontal to a vertical form, whenever firms were not able to secure nearby buildings to accommodate a larger number of workers. As the urban geographer James Vance writes:

> For the financial district [the] mechanical lift was of critical importance, because much of the movement tended to be internal to a rather clearly defined group of employees in a single organization or in a modest number of commonly related organizations. In that situation the walking zone limits could be reached within a few adjacent buildings, as in the structures built to house a legal community, a medical one, or even a very large single insurance company ... It seems to me not at all a matter of chance that the earliest skyscrapers to be built, those in New York and Chicago, were constructed predominantly for insurance companies and were among the earliest buildings to be equipped with elevators. Large metropolitan newspapers were other early entrants into the construction of skyscrapers, again finding a great advantage in piling large numbers of workers on top of each other and thus, by elevator, being able to secure rapid personal communication.[6]

The introduction of internal transportation also had expressive effects. Thus, the apartment buildings that were constructed prior to the elevator, in Paris for example, displayed a clear vertical stratification in which the social status of the inhabitants decreased with height. After the elevator was introduced, this stratification of regions was reversed, with apartments higher up expressing increased status.[7] Other expressive components vary with the activities housed by the building. In the case of residential buildings, the distinctive furniture of their internal regions and the decorative treatment of walls, floors and ceilings, have often played a role in the marking of social-class territories. Ostentatious displays in the aristocratic homes of Renaissance Italy, as Braudel reminds us, were in fact a way of using luxury as a means of domination. But as he goes on to argue, this luxury was purely expressive, since until many centuries later it was not associated with any kind of material comfort.[8] In the case of public buildings, particularly important examples are cathedrals, churches, mosques and synagogues: locales used for worshipping services, processions and religious ceremonies. These buildings must demarcate a sacred territory from a profane one through the expressive use of geometry and proportion. In medieval Europe, for example, the overall cruciform shape, arcaded cloisters and rhythmic patterns in stained-glass windows were all sacred territorial markers. No doubt, these spatial expressions often coexisted with religious representations. The fan-vaults of some English Gothic churches, for instance, with their series of ribs radiating upwards, express an expansive, ascending motion well suited to mark a sacred territory. This physical expression, of course, must work in conjunction with linguistic ones (the belief that, for example, heaven is above the earth), but it is not reducible to them.

What are the processes that stabilize or destabilize the identity of these assemblages? In the Chinese, Indian and Islamic civilizations, as well as among the European poor, the weight of tradition seems to have been almost overwhelmingly stabilizing when it comes to building techniques and materials, as well as the evolution of furniture and other elements of interior decoration. This evolution, when it took place, occurred at a glacial pace. The birth of *fashion*, on the other hand, had deterritorializing effects, although these were at first confined to the European rich. Fashion greatly accelerated the pace at which the interior and exterior decoration of buildings evolved, although it was not until the 1700s that the rate of change approximated the speed to which we have become accustomed today.[9] The impetus behind fashion was not just the desire to mark social-class territories through the way bodies and homes were dressed but also derived from the fact that, in Europe, aristocracies saw their distinguishing expressive markers constantly under threat by the increased social mobility of rich merchants and artisans. This resulted in a spiralling 'arms race' that drove change. As Braudel writes:

> I have always thought that fashion resulted to a large extent from the desire of the privileged to distinguish themselves, whatever the cost, from the masses that followed; to set up a barrier … Pressure from followers and imitators obviously made the pace quicken. And if this was the case, it was because prosperity granted privileges to a certain number of *nouveaux riches* and pushed them to the fore.[10]

Another process deterritorializing the identity of buildings is drastic changes in the routines which give them a temporal rhythm. In the case of organizations possessing an authority structure, changes in either practices of legitimization or enforcement may affect the identity of locales. As new enforcement routines replaced old ones in the seventeenth and eighteenth centuries, for example, they generated a distinct regionalization and connectivity in the buildings of factories, prisons, hospitals and schools. As Michel Foucault writes, these buildings have

> an architecture that is no longer built simply to be seen (as with ostentatious palaces), or to observe the external space (cf. the geometry of fortresses), but to permit an internal, articulated and detailed control – to render visible those who are inside it ... The old simple schema of confinement and enclosure – thick walls, a heavy gate that prevents entering or leaving – began to be replaced by the calculation of openings, of filled and empty spaces, passages and transparencies.[11]

We can extend these remarks to other types of locales, such as office buildings. The bodies of bureaucrats, for example, must also be analytically distributed in space, pinned down to their offices, and separated from any activity not directly related to their jobs. 'The physical separation of offices', Giddens writes, 'insulates each from the other and gives a measure of autonomy to those within them, and also serves as a powerful marker of hierarchy.'[12]

The changes brought about by fashion, or by the disciplinary use of space, already point to the fact that buildings exist in collectivities of similar assemblages, since in both cases we are concerned with how new forms propagate over time through an entire population. These populations of buildings, in turn, form larger assemblages such as residential neighbourhoods, commercial, industrial or government districts, or even moral (or immoral) zones, such as red-light districts. What components play a material or expressive role in these larger assemblages? On the material side, we must list all the physical locales defining stations for the periodic intersection of the life paths of neighbours (the local square, churches, pubs, shops) as well as the streets providing the necessary connectivity among them. A whole underground infrastructure, starting with water and sewage pipes and conduits for the gas that powered early street lighting, was added in the nineteenth century, and the twentieth contributed with electricity cables and telephone wires.

On the expressive side, it was the exterior of buildings, that is, the decoration (or lack of it) of their facades, that defined the personality of a neighbourhood. In residential neighbourhoods where streets were narrow and their layout formed a complex maze, the frontage of houses remained rather plain. Hence, expressive exteriors appear first in public buildings. These were typically located on a central square in which the surrounding space opened up vistas, that is, opportunities for unusual visual experiences, and effect enhanced by a straight street leading to the church, administrative building or monument. Aristocratic residential buildings joined public ones by the fifteenth century, as the European rich began deliberately to pick observable sites for the location of private houses. Only when enough space was left open around these buildings could expressive ostentation, and the interclass competition that fuelled it, begin to touch the external surfaces.[13] Besides opening up vistas, the central square of a town played another expressive role: as a centre determining the location of residential neighbourhoods, with proximity to it expressing greater social prestige. This concentric arrangement was characteristic of many European medieval towns, but was more prevalent south of the Alps. In the north, where merchants or craftsmen dominated their settlements, a market-place occupied the centre of the city, and accessibility to it determined the desirability of a location. This functional rather than social separation led to a more egalitarian form of expressivity, particularly in those planned towns named '*bastides*' which were used in the late Middle Ages as a means to colonize economically backward areas within Europe.[14]

Next we must list the processes that sharpen the boundaries and increase the internal homogeneity of a given neighbourhood. The processes of *congregation and segregation* are among those that perform this territorializing function. As James Vance writes:

> The activities that grow up in cities show a strong tendency to come together in limited areas of specialization drawn into a congregation by the internalizing linkages among them. Whether it be the use of shared sources of materials, the selling to a common body of customers, the practice of a given religion, or the speaking of a particular language, the institutional practice shapes the process of congregation, which is internally induced and highly responsive to matters of scale. A few persons doing a particular thing normally congregate, but not in an obvious congregation. When numbers are

increased to the point that they present an areally extensive pattern, then a geographical congregation is to be seen ... In contrast to a congregation is a similarly extensive grouping of ostensibly similar individuals induced by external forces. Instead of being drawn together, they are forced together by segregation.[15]

Commercial and industrial neighbourhoods have often been subject to the processes of congregation and segregation: similar crafts and trades have traditionally tended to congregate, while certain noxious activities like slaughtering have often been the target of institutional segregation. But residential neighbourhoods too acquire relatively well-defined borders, and a uniform internal composition, through these processes. The case of institutionalized segregation is perhaps the clearest example, since in this case both the boundaries and composition of a neighbourhood are codified by law and enforced by government organizations. But congregation may also result in a relatively homogenous composition (by race, ethnic group, class, language) even when one assumes a desire by residents to live in a relatively integrated neighbourhood. If people who do not actively discriminate also prefer not to be in the minority, whether relative to their immediate neighbours or relative to their overall proportion in the neighbourhood, there will be critical thresholds in the composition of a neighbourhood beyond which a chain reaction takes place causing a flight away from the locale by one of the groups.[16]

Important examples of processes of deterritorialization are increased *geographical mobility* and the effect of *land rents* on the allocation of uses for a particular neighbourhood or district. As the sociologists who pioneered urban studies pointed out long ago, segregation sharpens the boundaries of residential areas, whereas transportation tends to blur them.[17] A good example of the destabilizing effects of the increased mobility afforded by mechanical transportation are the changes that working-class neighbourhoods underwent towards the end of the nineteenth century. These neighbourhoods had sharply defined borders when the journey to work was on foot, but as the electric trolley became available the need to live near the factory was removed and new working-class suburbs with more porous boundaries emerged. Vance summarizes the situation thus:

The fundamental assemblage of buildings and uses in the English industrial city was the working class district composed of row housing ranged around one or several factories and served by quite local shops and pubs. The locating factor was the factory, because the hours of labour were long and the virtually universal way of going to work was on foot. The result was the creation of a city, or even a metropolis, of small, very definite neighbourhoods, which contained the life of most people save for weekly or less frequent visits to the market square, the market hall, or the street market for the buying of items of clothing, house furnishings, or perishable food. This parochial existence was enforced by conditions of work and housing and the economic unavailability of access to mechanical transportation. Only later in the nineteenth century, when the bicycle, the trolley, and finally the cheap excursion to the seaside by train began to come into the life of the working class, did any appreciable breaking out of this narrow geographical frame of life occur.[18]

Increased geographical mobility, in turn, interacted with the way in which land-assignment and land-use were determined to produce more drastic changes in the identity of neighbourhoods. Central authorities have always had a say in these allocative decisions, and they still do, their zoning regulations having a territorializing effect. Land-rents, on the other hand, when they became sufficiently fluid to give rise to economic speculation, were a powerful deterritorializing force, divorcing the reasons for land-ownership from any consideration of the activities taking place in it and promoting the relatively rapid displacement of one land-use by another. Early urban sociologists referred to this phenomenon as *land-succession*, after the ecological process in which a given assemblage of plants gives way to another assemblage as an ecosystem grows towards its climax mix of vegetation. Instead of plants these sociologists were concerned with land-uses and modelled this succession as a concentric expansion away from a city's centre. The core was taken over by a central business district, encircled by a zone in transition, with light manufacture and deteriorating residential neighbourhoods. Next came a ring of working-class neighbourhoods, followed by middle- and upper-class neighbourhoods, and finally the suburbs or the commuters' zone.[19]

Those early studies, however, focused on a single city (Chicago) and did not give a full explanation of the mechanisms involved in succession. The concentric-ring model seems to be valid for many cities in the USA, where incomes do tend to rise with distance from a city's centre, but not for many parts of Continental Europe, where the reverse is the case.[20]

This may explained by the older age of European cities and the fact that, as I mentioned before, proximity to the centre was very prestigious earlier in their history. At the core, the displacement of residential by commercial uses in the nineteenth century was a kind of territorial invasion which produced the central shopping district. While a wholesaler's location was determined by proximity to the port or the railroad station, the location of retail shops became increasingly determined by the intensity of pedestrian traffic and the convergence of transportation lines.[21] Having conquered its territory near the centre, retail itself differentiated into specialty shops (with more locational freedom) and commodity-combining shops, such as the centrally located department store, the first example of which emerged in Paris in the 1850s.[22] In addition, retailing had to compete with activities involving the exchange of information – as it occurs among brokers, bankers, couriers and other traffickers of knowledge – and its shops with the office space sought out by these service providers. Eventually, taller buildings decreased the intensity of the competition by giving the territory a vertical differentiation, with shops occupying the first floor and offices those higher up.

Explaining the process of land-succession already involves going beyond individual neighbourhoods to a consideration of populations or collectivities of neighbourhoods interacting with one another. Moreover, since these interactions depend on the relative location of members of these populations with respect to a central locale, land-succession implies the existence of larger assemblages of which neighbourhoods and districts are component parts: towns and cities. The identity of these larger assemblages, in turn, may be affected by the succession processes taking place within them. As I argued above, the centre of a city, particularly when there is a single one, is a privileged locale which plays a large role in defining its identity. A central square may owe its location to the building which served as a nucleus for the urban settlement, a church or a castle, for example, and to this extent may serve as an expression of the historical origins of the town. Likewise, when the centre is occupied by a market-place, the commercial character of the town is expressed by that very fact. Thus, when a city loses its *mono centricity* its historical identity may be affected. This multiplication of centres occurred in many countries after 1945 as suburbanization and the increased use of automobiles made the city's core a less promising place for retail activities, and as shopping centres in outlying locations became increasingly common.

But even before the proliferation of suburbs and industrial hinter-lands, the identity of urban settlements depended on their relationship with their surroundings. Until relatively recently this meant the countryside and its rural villages. A town may emerge within a pre-existing rural area, a process referred to as *synoecism*, or on the contrary, it may be planted in an area lacking previous rural inhabitants with urban life projected outwards on surrounding areas, a process called *dioecism*.[23] But whether it is through a rural implosion or an urban explosion that the difference between town and countryside is established, it is this difference that constitutes them both, a difference in their mix of routine activities and in their density of population. The distinction of routine activities is based on the oldest form of division of labour: that between agricultural activities on the one hand, and those of commerce, industry and formal government on the other. Until the last two centuries, this separation of activities was not abruptly discontinuous: towns kept vegetable gardens and raised farm animals within their walls, while rural villages engaged in small-scale industry.[24] The distinction in terms of demographic density also varied in sharpness, but it was always there, however blurred. Some big villages may have been larger than some small towns, but the latter always packed more people into the same amount of space.

The relations between town and countryside may be characterized in terms of the resources with which they supply one another. A medieval town of 3,000 inhabitants, for example, needed the land of about ten villages (or 8.5 kilometres) to generate enough food for its inhabitants.[25] But those villages, in turn, needed services from the town, from the commercial services provided by its market-place to the legal, medical, financial and educational services supplied by its organizations, as well as the military protection afforded by its walls and armies. Yet, despite the mutuality of resource dependencies, cities have always tended to dominate the countryside because of the cumulative, *self-stimulating dynamics* that characterize them. There are many models of these dynamics, some stressing the mutual stimulation between the accumulation of workers in a place and the availability of economic investment, private or public, in that place; others focusing on the mutual stimulation between different economic activities that supply each other with materials and services and provide demand for each other's products. In all models, however, 'spatial concentration itself creates the favourable economic environment that supports further or continued concentration'.[26] These self-stimulating dynamics can make towns grow much faster than their countryside, increasing their influence and breaking the symmetry of the resource dependencies.

In fact, an assemblage analysis of urban centres must take into account not only town and countryside, but also the geographical region they both occupy. This region is an important source of components playing a material role in the assemblage. The geographical site and situation of a given urban settlement provides it with a range of objective opportunities and risks, the exploitation and avoidance of which depends on interactions between social entities (persons, networks, organizations) and physical and chemical ones (rivers, oceans, topsoil, mineral deposits). In addition to ecological components there are those making up the infrastructure of a city, that is, its physical form and its connectivity. While the physical form of some towns may result from a mere aggregation of its neighbourhoods, some aspects of its connectivity (those related to citywide mechanical transportation) tend to have properties of their own, and are capable of affecting the form of the neighbourhoods themselves. The best example is perhaps that of locomotives. Their large mass made them hard to stop as well as to accelerate again, and this demanded the construction of elevated or underground tracks whenever they had to intermesh with pedestrian traffic. The same physical constraints determined an interval of two or three miles between train stops, directly influencing the spatial distribution of the suburbs which grew around railroad stations, giving this distribution its characteristic beadlike shape.[27]

The components playing an expressive role in an urban assemblage may also be a mere aggregation of those of its neighbourhoods, or go beyond these. Let's take for example the silhouette which the mass of a town's residential houses and buildings, as well as the decorated tops of its churches and public buildings, cut against the sky. In some cases, this *skyline* is a mere aggregate effect, but the rhythmic repetition of architectural motifs – belfries and steeples, minarets, domes and spires, even smokestacks, water-towers and furnace cones – and the way these motifs play in counterpoint with the surrounding features of the landscape, may result in a whole that is more than a simple sum.[28] Either way, skylines, however humble, greeted for centuries the eyes of incoming people at the different approaches to a city, constituting a kind of visual signature of its territorial identity. This was particularly true before the blurring of city boundaries by suburbs and industrial hinterlands, but cities endowed with large skyscrapers continue to possess this physical expressivity even in these new conditions. In some cases, however, as the architectural historian Spiro Kostoff reminds us, the process through which old and new skylines become territorial signatures involve a variety of visual representations, such as those found in coins, paintings and prints aimed at tourists.[29]

The processes that stabilize a city's identity concern both the sharpness of its physical borders as well as the routine human practices taking place within those borders, in particular, the form taken by *residential practices*. In ancient Greek towns, for example, a substantial part of the population returned to their rural homes in summer months or in times of economic trouble. This custom, in turn, affected the process of congregation that formed neighbourhoods within towns: residents tended to congregate by their rural place of origin and maintained their geographic loyalties.[30] In addition, military threats made the inhabitants of a Greek town disperse rather than hide behind its walls. This combination of factors resulted in towns that, in a sense, blended with their countrysides and therefore did not have a sharply defined identity. The opposite case is exemplified by medieval European towns, where fortified walls provided not only protection for the rural population during a siege but also a sense of security against undefined outsiders: a sense which, even in the absence of overt conflict, helped to make citizens into clearly defined insiders. In addition, the stone walls marked the point beyond which the exclusivity of citizenship and its privileges ended, unlike the Greek case in which citizenship could be held by those who practised a duality of residence. Overall, medieval towns had a much sharper identity as locales. These cities, as Braudel writes, 'were the West's first focus of patriotism – and the patriotism they inspired was long to be more coherent and much more conscious than the territorial kind, which emerged only slowly in the first states'.[31]

The native town in ancient Greece and the walled medieval town represent two extreme forms which city boundaries may take. An interesting intermediate case was created by the rise of the suburb in the nineteenth century, and its proliferation in the twentieth. Whereas at first suburbs and industrial hinterlands simply blurred the outer boundaries of cities which otherwise retained their centre, and hence their old identity, after the Second World War not only the area which suburbs occupied but the variety of their land-uses (retail, wholesale, manufacturing and office space) multiplied, recreating the complex combinations that used to characterize the old central business district. As I noted before, this process created brand new centres in the suburban band. In some cases, the urban realms around these centres were so self-sufficient that the daily paths of their residents could be contained within their limits.[32] Thus, by creating a true multi-centred urban space, suburban growth – and the changes in connectivity brought about by the automobile and the freeway – acted as a powerful deterritorializing force.

As usual, an assemblage analysis of singular, individual entities must be complemented by a study of the populations formed by those entities. An important property of populations of towns and cities is the birth-rate of new urban settlements, as well as the rate at which old settlements disappear. These determine the overall *rate of urbanization* of a particular geographical region. In the case of Europe, urbanization intensified in the eleventh and twelfth centuries, accelerated again in the sixteenth, and picked up speed once more in the centuries following the Industrial Revolution. Between 1350 and 1450, and between 1650 and 1750, both the human population and the overall rate of urbanization declined.[33] The first wave of city-building took place against the background of feudalism, creating densely occupied areas in which a certain autonomy from feudal relations could be achieved – the city's land still belonged to a bishop or a prince, but the city as a whole paid the rent – as well as areas with lower urban density in which cities could not shed their shackles.

Higher density affected not only the relations of cities with feudal organizations, making them more contractual and less directly tributary, but also the intensity of the economic interactions between cities. In the period between the years 1000 and 1300, cities in the low-density feudal areas (Spain, France, England) did not develop systematic relations among themselves, remaining within relatively closed politico-economic domains in which trade relationships were mostly local. In the high-density areas (northern Italy, Flanders, the Netherlands, some parts of Germany), on the other hand, the regularity of trade was greater, its volume higher, and it covered much larger areas. This led to the generation of more systematic and enduring relations among urban centres creating the conditions for the emergence of larger assemblages: hierarchies and networks of cities. Much as the differentiation between a city and its surrounding countryside involved breaking the symmetry of its resource dependencies through self-stimulating accumulations, other cumulative processes – related to differential degrees of autonomy from feudal organizations, the relative speed of different forms of transportation, differences in volume and intensity of trade – destroyed the possibility of a uniformly sized population of towns with symmetric resource dependencies.

In formal models of urban dynamics, assemblages of cities of different sizes emerge from a sequence of symmetry-breaking events, as each town confronts centripetal processes, like the capture of population, investment and other resources, as well as centrifugal ones, like congestion, pollution, traffic. At the tipping-point, when one set of forces begins to dominate the other, a town may grow explosively or shrink to a small size in the shadow of a larger one.[34] In computer simulations the actual pattern that emerges *is not unique* – as if there existed a single optimal pattern to which the urban dynamics always tended – but is, on the contrary, highly sensitive to the actual historical sequence of events. For this reason, the emergent pattern of urban centres is like a memory of this symmetry-breaking sequence 'fossilized in the spatial structure of the system'.[35]

A recurrent emergent pattern in these formal models is one familiar to geographers: a hierarchy of *central places*. In its original formulation, central-place theory was an attempt to describe the hierarchical relations among regularly spaced urban centres, with larger ones displaying a greater degree of service differentiation than smaller ones. In the hierarchies that emerged in medieval Europe, for example, the smallest towns offered a small market-place and a church as services to their rural surroundings; medium-sized towns added to this marketing function more elaborate religious services, as well as some simple administrative and educational ones, such as county jails and schools, which they offered to their countrysides as well as to lower-ranked towns. Larger towns, in turn, multiplied the variety of marketing, administrative and religious services and added new ones, such as the sophisticated educational services provided by universities.[36] In short, in a central-place hierarchy each rank offers all the services of the immediately lower rank and a few more, and these added services create resource dependencies across ranks. To these it must be added the economic dependencies which trade may create, since larger towns typically offered a larger variety of products than smaller ones, as well as political dependencies derived from the fact that the largest towns at the top of the hierarchy were usually regional or provincial capitals. In addition to landlocked central-place hierarchies, trade among the European population of towns in the Middle Ages generated extensive *networks of maritime ports* in which cities were not geographically fixed centres but changing relays, junctions or outposts. As the urban historians Hohenberg and Lees write:

Instead of a hierarchical nesting of similar centres, distinguished mainly by the number and rarity of services offered, [a maritime network] presents an ordering of functionally complementary cities and urban settlements. The key systemic property of a city is nodality rather than centrality, whereas hierarchical differences derive only partly from size and more from the nature of the dominant urban function. Control and innovation confer the most power and status, followed by transmission of goods and messages, and finally by execution of routine production tasks. Since network cities easily exercise control at a distance, the influence of a town has little to do with propinquity and even less with formal control over territory.[37]

Each node in these networks specialized on a subset of economic activities not shared with the rest, with the dominant nodes typically monopolizing those that yielded the most profits. Since rates of profit vary historically, as sources of supply change or as fashion switches demand from one luxury product to another, the mix of activities in each node of the network also changed, and this, in turn, affected the dominance relations between nodes. For this reason, the position of dominant node, or 'core', as it is sometimes referred to, changed over time, although it was always occupied by a powerful maritime port. The sequence of cities occupying the core was roughly this: Venice was dominant in the fourteenth century, followed by Antwerp in the fifteenth, Genoa in the sixteenth, Amsterdam in the seventeenth, London in the next two centuries, and New York in the twentieth.[38] Besides economic specialization, Hohenberg and Lees mention control at a distance as a characteristic of city networks, a relative independence from spatial proximity made possible by the much higher speed of transportation by sea relative to that over land. Faster transportation implied that nodes in the network were in a sense closer to each other than to the landlocked cities in their own backyard: news, goods, money, people, even contagious deceases, all travelled more rapidly from node to node than they did from one central place to another.

As assemblages, central-place hierarchies and maritime networks have different components playing material and expressive roles. Materially, they vary in both geographical situation and connectivity. On the one hand, the geographical siting of central places always gave them command over land resources, farmland in particular. By contrast, the cities in maritime networks, particularly the dominant nodes, were relatively poor in these terms: Venice was so ecologically deprived it was condemned to trade from the start, and Amsterdam had to be constantly reclaiming land from the sea. In terms of connectivity, roads linked central places following the ranks of the hierarchy: there were seldom direct land-routes connecting the smaller towns to the regional capital. Also, the relative slowness of terrestrial transportation forced towns to cluster together, since the services offered by larger centres could only be enjoyed if the smaller ones were located at relatively short distances: the distance its inhabitants would be willing to walk to get the needed service. Maritime ports were not subject to these constraints. Not only were long distances less of a problem, given the faster speed of their ships, but they could all be directly connected to one another regardless of rank. The key to this connectivity was the sea. During the first wave of urbanization, for instance, 'the two inland seas, the Mediterranean–Adriatic and the Channel–North Sea–Baltic, served to unite trading centres rather than to separate them'.[39] After that, first the Atlantic Ocean, and later on the Pacific, became the connecting waters of a network that by the seventeenth century had acquired global proportions.

While the expressive components of these assemblages may be a mere aggregate of those of the towns that are their component parts, the aggregate may have a pattern of its own. In the case of central places, if we imagine travelling from the smallest and simplest towns up the ranks until we reach the regional capital, this experience would reveal a pattern of increased complexity in the expressive elements giving towns their personality: taller and more decorated churches and central plazas, more lavish religious and secular ceremonies, a greater variety of street and workshop activities, as well as more diversified and colourful market-places. In the case of maritime networks, it was not the increased differentiation of one and the same regional culture that expressed a dominant position but the gathering of expressions from all over the world. The core cities, in particular, always had the highest cost of living and the highest rate of inflation, so every commodity from around the world, however exotic, tended to flow towards their high prices. 'These world-cities put all their delights on display', writes Braudel, becoming universal warehouses, inventories of the possible, veritable Noah's Arks.[40]

Territorialization in these assemblages is performed by the processes that give an entire region a certain homogeneity. The largest central places, often playing the role of political capitals, attracted talented people from the lower-ranked towns: people who brought with them linguistic and nonlinguistic elements of their own local culture. Over time, these capitals gathered, elaborated and synthesized these elements into a more or less homogenous product which was then re-exported back to the smaller centres.[41] The *higher prestige* of the more differentiated culture at the top acted as a magnet for the short-distance migratory patterns of cultural producers, and gave the synthesized cultural product the means to propagate throughout the region. Long-distance trade, on the other hand, had deterritorializing effects. The nodes of a maritime network often played the role of *gateways to the outside*, opening up to foreign civilizations, so they housed a more colourful and varied population. Having a larger proportion of foreign merchants than did the central places, maritime ports offered their inhabitants the opportunity to be in more regular contact with outsiders and their alien manners, dress and ideas. The existence of dominant nodes implies that the more cosmopolitan culture of urban networks was not egalitarian, but its heterogeneity was preserved since it was 'superimposed on a traditional periphery with no attempt at integration or gradual synthesis'.[42]

Moving from the scale of city assemblages to that of territorial states may be done in an abstract way, simply noting that the landlocked regions organized by central-place hierarchies and the coastal regions structured by maritime networks are today component parts of nation-states. But this would leave out the historical process behind the absorption of cities into larger entities, as well as the resistance offered by urban centres to such an integration. In Europe, the outcome of this process varied, depending on the segment of the population of cities that was involved. In the densely urbanized regions cities managed to slow down the crystallization of territorial states until the nineteenth century, while in the areas of low density they were quickly absorbed. In particular, unlike the central-place hierarchies just examined, those that emerged in the areas where feudalism remained dominant tended to adopt distorted forms with excessively large cities at the top. These disproportionately populous and powerful centres formed the nucleus around which empires, kingdoms and nation-states grew by a slow accretion of territory, and, in time, they became the national capitals of these larger assemblages.

Although the incorporation of cities in the sixteenth and seventeenth centuries was performed through a variety of means, direct military interventions were often involved. In some cases the rulers of kingdoms or empires made claims to the territory on which cities were located: claims legitimated by inheritance or marriage but often enforced through the use of organized violence. But warfare also influenced the outcome of the contest between cities and territorial states indirectly through the enormous expense that armies and fortified frontiers implied. Only large, centralized governments, commanding the entire resources of a land and its inhabitants, could afford to stay in the arms races that developed between new weapons (such as mobile artillery) and defensive fortifications. As the historian Paul Kennedy writes:

> Military factors – or better, geostrategical factors – helped to shape the territorial boundaries of these new nation-states, while the frequent wars induced national consciousness, in a negative fashion at least, in that Englishman learned to hate Spaniards, Swedes to hate Danes, Dutch rebels to hate their former Habsburg overlords. Above all, it was war – and especially the new techniques which favoured the growth of infantry armies and expensive fortifications and fleets – which impelled belligerent states to spend more money than ever before, and to seek a corresponding amount in revenues . . . In the last few years of Elizabeth's England, or in Phillip II's Spain, as much as three-quarters of all government expenditures was devoted to war or to debt repayments for previous wars. Military and naval endeavors may not always have been the *raison d'être* of the new nation-states, but it certainly was their most expensive and pressing activity.[43]

The historical period that sealed the fate of autonomous cities can be framed by two critical dates, 1494 and 1648, a period that witnessed warfare increasing enormously in both intensity and geographical scope. The first date marks the year when the Italian city-states were first invaded and brought to their knees by armies from beyond the Alps: the French armies under Charles VIII whose goal was to enforce territorial claims on the kingdom of Naples. The second date celebrates the signing of the peace treaty of Westphalia, ending the Thirty Years War between the largest territorial entity at the time, the Catholic Habsburg empire, and an alliance between France, Sweden and a host of Protestant-aligned states. When the peace treaty was finally signed by the exhausted participants, a unified, geopolitically stabilizing Germany had been created at the centre of Europe, and the frontiers that defined the identity of territorial states, as well as the balance of power between them, were consolidated. Although the crucial legal concept of 'sovereignty' had been formalized prior to the war (by Jean Bodin in 1576) it was during the peace conference that it was first used in practice to define the identity of territorial states as legal entities.[44] Thus, international law may be said to have been the offspring of that war.

As I argued in the previous chapter, it is important not to confuse territorial states as *geopolitical entities* with the organizational hierarchies that govern them. Geopolitical factors are properties of the former but not of the latter. As Paul Kennedy argues, given the fact that after 1648 warfare typically involved many national actors, geography affected the fate of a nation not merely through

> such elements as a country's climate, raw materials, fertility of agriculture, and access to trade routes – important though they all were to its overall prosperity – but rather [via] the critical issue of strategical *location* during these multilateral wars. Was a particular nation able to concentrate its energies upon one front, or did it have to fight on several? Did it share common borders with weak states, or powerful ones? Was it chiefly a land power, a sea power, or a hybrid – and what advantages and disadvantages did that bring? Could it easily pull out of a great war in Central Europe if it wished to? Could it secure additional resources from overseas?[45]

But if territorial states cannot be reduced to their civilian and military organizations, the latter do form the main actors whose routine activities give these largest of regionalized locales their temporal structure. A good example of the new organizational activities that were required after 1648 were the fiscal and monetary policies, as well as the overall system of public finance, needed to conduct large-scale warfare. On the economic side there were activities guided by a heterogeneous body of pragmatic beliefs referred to as 'mercantilism'. The central belief of this doctrine was that the wealth of a nation was based on the amount of precious metals (gold and silver) that accumulated within its borders. This monetary policy, it is clear today, is based on mistaken beliefs about the causal relations between economic factors. On the other hand, since one means of preventing the outward flow of precious metals was to discourage imports, and this, in turn, involved the promotion of local manufacture and of internal economic growth, mercantilism had collective unintended consequences that did benefit territorial states in the long run.[46] For this reason, however, it is hard to consider the people making mercantilist policy decisions the relevant social actors in this case. Another reason to consider the activities of organizations the main source of temporal structure for territorial states is that many of the capacities necessary to conduct a sound fiscal policy were the product of *slow organizational learning*, a feat first achieved in England between the years of 1688 and 1756. As Braudel writes:

> This financial revolution which culminated in a transformation of public credit was only made possible by a previous thoroughgoing remodeling of the kingdom's finances along clearly defined lines. Generally speaking, in 1640 and still in 1660, English financial structures were very similar to those of France. On neither side of the Channel did centralized public finance, under the exclusive control of the state, exist. Too much had been abandoned to the private initiative of tax-collectors, who were at the same time official money lenders, to financiers who had their own affairs in mind, and to officeholders who did not depend on the state since they had purchased their posts, not to mention the constant appeals that were made to the City of London, just as the king of France was always calling on the goodwill of Paris. The English reform, which consisted in getting rid of parasitic intermediaries, was accomplished steadily and with discretion, *though without any discernible plan of action.*[47]

An assemblage analysis of organizational hierarchies has already been sketched in the previous chapter, so what remains to be analysed is the territorial states themselves. Among the components playing a material role we must list all the resources contained within a country's frontiers, not only its natural resources (agricultural land and mineral deposits of coal, oil, precious metals) but also its demographic ones, that is, its human populations viewed as reservoirs of army and navy recruits as well as of potential taxpayers. As with all locales, the material aspect also involves questions of connectivity between regions: questions that in this case involve the geographical regions previously organized by cities. Territorial states did not create these regions, nor the provinces that several such regions formed, but they did affect their interconnection through the building of new roads and canals. This is how, for example, Britain stitched together several provincial markets to create the first national market in the eighteenth century, a process in which its national capital played a key centralizing role. And, as Braudel argues, without the national market 'the modern state would be a pure fiction'.[48]

Other countries (France, Germany, the USA) accomplished this feat in the following century through the use of locomotives and telegraphs. The advent of steam endowed land transportation with the speed it had lacked for so long, changing the balance of power between landlocked and coastal regions and their cities, and giving national capitals a dominant position. With the rise of railroads, as Hohenberg and Lees write, although

> many traditional nodes and gateways continued to flourish, the pull of territorial capitals on trade, finance, and enterprise could grow unchecked. With their concentration of power and wealth, these cities commanded the design of rail networks and later of the motorways, and so secured the links on which future nodality depended. Where once the trade routes and waterways had determined urban locations and roles in the urban network, rail transportation now accommodated the expansion needs of the great cities for both local traffic and distant connections.[49]

On the expressive side, the most important example was the use of national capitals as a means to display central control. This was achieved through the so-called 'Grand Manner' of urban design pioneered in Europe by the absolutist governments of the seventeenth and eighteenth centuries. Italian cities created the basic elements of the Grand Manner, but it was in France after 1650 that these elements became codified into a style: residential blocks with uniform facades acting as frames for sweeping vistas which culminated with an obelisk, triumphal arch, or statue, acting as a visual marker; long and wide tree-lined avenues; a use of the existing or modified topography for dramatic effect; and the coordination of all these elements into grand geometric configurations.[50] Although the use of symbols and visual representations was also part of this global approach to urban design, it can be argued that the overall theatricality of the Grand Manner, and its carefully planned manipulation of a city's visual experience, physically expressed the concentration of power. To quote Spiro Kostoff:

If the Grand Manner is routinely associated with centralized power, we can readily see why. The very expansiveness it calls for, and the abstraction of its patterns, presuppose an untangled decision-making process and the wherewithal to accomplish what has been laid out. When such clearcut authority cannot be had the Grand Manner remains on paper ... It was not an accident that Washington was the only American city to celebrate the Grand Manner unequivocally ... This was the only city in the United States that had a centralized administration, however deputized, being under direct authority of Congress. Elsewhere one could only resort to persuasion, and try to advance whatever fragments of the overall plan one could through the tangles of the democratic process ... The presumption of absolute power explains the appeal of the Grand Manner for the totalitarian regimes of the Thirties – for the likes of Mussolini, Hitler and Stalin.[51]

The stability of the identity of territorial states depends in part on the degree of uniformity (ethnic, religious, linguistic, monetary, legal) that its organizations and cities manage to create within its borders. A good example of homogenization at this scale is the creation of standard languages. In the areas which had been latinized during the Roman Empire, for example, each central place hierarchy had its own dominant dialect, the product of the divergent evolution that spoken or vulgar Latin underwent after the imperial fall. Before the rise of national capitals the entire range of romance dialects that resulted from this divergent differentiation coexisted, even as some cities accumulated more prestige for their own versions. But as territorial states began to consolidate their grip, the balance of power changed. In some cases, special organizations (official language academies) were created to codify the dialects of the dominant capitals and to publish official dictionaries, grammars and books of correct pronunciation. This codification, however, did not manage to propagate the new artificial languages throughout the entire territory. That process had to wait until the nineteenth century for the creation of a nationwide system of compulsory elementary education in the standard. Even then, many regions and their cities resisted this imposition and managed to preserve their own linguistic identity, a resistance that was a source of centripetal forces. Although in some countries, such as Switzerland, political stability coexists with multi-lingualism, in others (Canada, Belgium) even bilingualism has proved to be a destabilizing force.[52]

In addition to internal uniformity, territorialization at this scale has a more direct spatial meaning: the stability of the defining frontiers of a country. This stability has two aspects, the control of the different flows moving across the border, and the endurance of the frontiers themselves. The latter refers to the fact that the annexation (or secession) of a large piece of land changes the geographical identity of a territorial state. Although these events need not involve warfare aimed at territorial expansion (or civil war aimed at secession) they often do, and this shows the importance of deploying armies near the border or constructing special fortifications for the consolidation of frontiers. A few decades after the treaty of Westphalia was signed, for example, France redirected enormous resources to the creation of coherent, defensible boundaries, through the systematic construction of fortress towns, perimeter walls and citadels – separate star-shaped strongholds sited next to a town's perimeter. In the hands of Sebastien le Prestre de Vauban, the brilliant military engineer, France's defining borders became nearly impregnable, maintaining their defensive value until the French Revolution. Vauban built double rows of fortresses in the northern and southeastern frontiers, so systematically related to each other that one 'would be within earshot of French fortress guns all the way from the Swiss border to the Channel'.[53]

Migration and trade across national borders tend to complicate the effort to create a single national identity, and to this extent they may be considered deterritorializing. The ability to reduce the permeability of frontiers depends to a large degree on the conditions under which a territorial entity comes into being. Those kingdoms and empires that crystallized in the feudal areas of Europe had an easier task creating internal homogeneity than those in the densely urbanized areas that had to cope with the split sovereignty derived from the coexistence of many autonomous city-states.[54] Similarly, territorial states born from the collapse of a previous empire or from the break-up of former colonial possessions can find themselves with unstable frontiers cutting across areas heterogeneous in language, ethnicity or religion: a situation which militates against a stable identity and complicates border control. A more systematic challenge to border control and territorial stability has existed since at least the seventeenth century. As the identity of the modern international system was crystallizing during the Thirty Years War, the city of Amsterdam had become the dominant centre of a transnational trade and credit network that was almost as global as anything that exists today. If the rise of kingdoms, empires and nation-states exerted territorializing pressures on cities by reducing their autonomy, maritime networks not only resisted these pressures but were capable then, and still are today, of deterritorializing the constitutive boundaries of territorial states. The pressure on these boundaries has intensified in recent decades as the ease with which financial resources can flow across state boundaries, the degree of differentiation of the international division of labour, and the mobility of legal and illegal workers, have all increased.

That networks of cities, and the transnational organizations based on those cities, can operate over, and give coherence to, large geographical areas cutting across state boundaries, has been recognized since the pioneering work of Fernand Braudel, who refers to these areas as 'world-economies'.[55] It is too early, however, to tell whether these world-economies are as real as the other regionalized locales that have been analysed in this chapter. Some of the processes that are supposed to endow these economic locales with coherence, such as the synchronized movement of prices across large geographical areas following long temporal rhythms (the so-called 'Kondratieff waves'), remain controversial. But what is clear even at this stage of our understanding is that approaches based on reductionist social ontologies do not do justice to the historical data. This is particularly true of macro-reductionist approaches, such as the so-called 'world-systems analysis' pioneered by Immanuel Wallerstein, in which Braudel's original idea is combined with theories of uneven exchange developed by Latin American theorists.[56] In Wallerstein's view, for example, only one valid unit of social analysis has existed since the end of the Thirty Years War, the entire 'world-system'. Explanations at the level of nation-states are viewed as illegitimate since the position of countries in the world-system determines their very nature.[57] An assemblage approach, on the other hand, is more compatible with Braudel's original idea. Although he does not use the concept of 'assemblage', he views social wholes as 'sets of sets', giving each differently scaled entity its own relative autonomy without fusing it with the others into a seamless whole.[58]

It has been the purpose of this book to argue the merits of such a nonreductionist approach, an approach in which every social entity is shown to emerge from the interactions among entities operating at a smaller scale. The fact that the emergent wholes react back on their components to constrain them and enable them does not result in a seamless totality. Each level of scale retains a relative autonomy and can therefore be a legitimate unit of analysis. Preserving the ontological independence of each scale not only blocks attempts at micro-reductionism (as in neoclassical economics) and macro-reductionism (as in world-systems analysis) but also allows the integration of the valuable insights that different social scientists have developed while working at a specific spatiotemporal scale, from the extremely short duration of the small entities studied by Erving Goffman to the extremely long duration of the large entities studied by Fernand Braudel. Assemblage theory supplies the framework where the voices of these two authors, and of the many others whose work has influenced this book, can come together to form a chorus that does not harmonize its different components but interlocks them while respecting their heterogeneity.

Notes

Introduction

1. Ian Hacking, *The Social Construction of What?* (Cambridge, MA: Harvard University Press, 1999), p. 103.
2. Ibid., p. 49.
3. For passages on assemblage theory, see Gilles Deleuze and Felix Guattari, *A Thousand Plateaus* (Minneapolis, MN: University of Minnesota Press, 1987), pp. 71, 88–91, 323–37, 503–5.
4. Manuel DeLanda, *Intensive Science and Virtual Philosophy* (London: Continuum, 2002).
5. Margaret Archer, *Realist Social Theory. The Morphogenetic Approach* (Cambridge: Cambridge University Press, 1995). Archer does a similar critique of sociological theories but speaks of 'conflation' rather than 'reduction'. My micro-reductionism, macro-reductionism and meso-reductionism are labelled 'downward conflation', 'upward conflation' and 'central conflation' by her.
6. Manuel DeLanda, *War in the Age of Intelligent Machines* (New York: Zone Books, 1991); Manuel DeLanda, *A Thousand Years of Non-Linear History* (New York: Zone Books, 1997).

Chapter 1

1. Howard Becker and Harry Elmer Barnes, *Social Thought from Lore to Science* (New York: Dover, 1961), pp. 677–8.
2. G.W.F. Hegel, *The Science of Logic* (Amherst, NY: Humanity Books, 1999), Volume 2, Book 2, p. 711. (Emphasis in the original).
3. 'Structure is not "external" to individuals: as memory traces, and as

instantiated in social practices, it is in a certain sense more "internal" than exterior to their activities in a Durkheimian sense' (Anthony Giddens, *The Constitution of Society* [Berkeley, CA: University of California Press, 1986]. p. 25).

4. Ibid., page 3.
5. Anthony Giddens, *Central Problems in Social Theory* (Berkeley, CA: University of California Press, 1979), p. 53.
6. Mario Bunge, *Causality and Modern Science* (New York: Dover, 1979), p. 156.
7. Gilles Deleuze and Claire Parnet, *Dialogues II* (New York: Columbia University Press, 2002), p. 55.
8. Gilles Deleuze, *Empiricism and Subjectivity* (New York: Columbia University Press, 1991), p. 98. Deleuze is here discussing a specific type of component, Humean ideas (and this is what the original quote refers to), but the point applies to any other type of component.
9. Thus Deleuze writes:

> What is an assemblage? It is a multiplicity which is made up of heterogeneous terms and which establishes liaisons, relations between them, across ages, sexes and reigns – different natures. Thus the assemblage's only unity is that of a co-functioning: it is a symbiosis, a 'sympathy'. It is never filiations which are important, but alliances, alloys; these are not successions, lines of descent, but contagions, epidemics, the wind. (Deleuze and Parnet, *Dialogues II*, p. 69)

The exclusion of lines of descent, such as they exist among organisms and even species, shows that he means to exclude the latter from the definition of an assemblage. In his work with Félix Guattari, Deleuze distinguishes between 'assemblages' on the one hand, and 'strata' on the other. Biological organisms and institutional organizations would be classified by them as strata. I will not retain this distinction here for reasons explained below in note 21.

10. Deleuze and Guattari use slightly different terminology. In particular, instead of 'material' and 'expressive' roles for components they talk of segments of 'content' and 'expression':

> We may draw some conclusions of the nature of Assemblages from this. On a first, horizontal axis, an assemblage comprises two segments, one of content, the other of expression. On the one hand it is a *machinic assemblage* of bodies, of actions and passions, and intermingling of bodies reacting to one another; on the other hand, it is a *collective assemblage of enunciation*, of acts and statements, of incorporeal transformations attributed to bodies. Then, on a vertical axis, the assemblage has both *territorial sides*, or reterritorialized sides, which stabilize it, and *cutting edges of deterritorialization*, which carry it away. (Gilles Deleuze and Félix Guattari, *A Thousand Plateaus* [Minneapolis, MN: University of Minnesota Press, 1987], p. 88)

With the exception of the term 'territorialization' I will avoid using any of this complex terminology in this book. Also, instead of two dimensions I use three, a manœuvre which allows me to get rid of the distinction between strata and assemblages, as explained in note 21.

11. This distinction between linguistic and nonlinguistic expression is somewhat obscured in the previous note by the reference to expressive components as 'collective assemblages of enunciation', unless one interprets it as referring not to the semantic content of statements, but to their illocutionary force, that is, to what they express as 'speech acts'. See Deleuze and Guattari, *A Thousand Plateaus*, p. 80.

At any rate, even if we interpret 'statement' this way, the definition of assemblage is still inconvenient in that it seems to apply only to social cases (unless one takes inorganic and biological entities as capable of producing statements) which goes directly against the idea that assemblage theory applies equally well to physics, biology and sociology. See also note 13.

12. Edwin C. Kemble, *Physical Science. Its Structure and Development* (Cambridge, MA: MIT Press, 1966), pp. 126–7.

13. Deleuze and Guattari, *A Thousand Plateaus*, p. 62. Deleuze and Guattari distinguish the substance and the form of the materiality and expressivity of assemblages. Materiality involves not merely substance but formed substance, and expressivity is not purely formal but it involves its own substance. The specialization of genes and words is then conceptualized as the separation between the substance and form of expression. In what follows I will not stick to this terminology. I will speak of physical or direct expressivity to refer to, for example, facial expressions or the expressivity of *behaviour*, and refer to language as a specialized medium of expression. But the reader should keep in mind that facial expressions are referred to by Deleuze and Guattari as 'substance of expression' and language as 'form of expression'. As they write: 'On the other hand, language becomes the new form of expression ... The substance involved is fundamentally vocal substance, which brings into play various organic elements: not only the larynx, but the mouth and lips, and the overall motricity of the face' (ibid., p. 61).

14. In addition, the processes which territorialize or deterritorialize genes and words should be included. The materiality of language, for example, becomes territorialized with the emergence of writing. But this spatial identity may become deterritorialized when carvings in stone or inked inscriptions on paper become modulations in electromagnetic fields, as in radio transmissions of spoken language, or television broadcasts of written language. Deterritorializations of the expressive part of language, that is, its semantic content, are trickier to conceptualize. Deleuze gives some indications of how this conceptualization may be pursued. In particular, he singles out certain semantic entities as playing a key role in these

processes: infinitive verbs, proper nouns, indefinite articles. See ibid., pp. 263–4.

15. Deleuze and Guattari refer to this synthesis of wholes out of components as a process of *double articulation* (ibid., pp. 40–41). (This process is said to synthesize strata not assemblages, but see below, note 21.)

16. Ibid., p. 316.

17. Historically, the ancient Greek cities, located far from their main contemporary empires, but not so far that they could not benefit from their advanced civilizations, may have supplied the conditions in which conversations between friends broke free from the rigidity of similar encounters elsewhere. See Gilles Deleuze and Félix Guattari, *What is Philosophy?* (New York: Columbia University Press, 1994), p. 87. The Greek case is in fact a combination of deterritorialization and decoding. Here Deleuze and Guattari stress the former, but I would argue that decoding is also involved.

18. Fernand Braudel, *The Perspective of the World* (New York: Harper & Row, 1979), pp. 280–82.

19. Ibid., pp. 282–4.

20. Ibid., p. 287.

21. This departs from Deleuze and Guattari's own version of assemblage theory since they define assemblages along two, nor three dimensions, but they are then forced to introduce two categories of actual entities, strata and assemblages. To use this opposition would unnecessarily complicate the presentation, particularly when the same objective may be achieved by adding a third dimension to the concept of assemblage. That they thought the opposition between strata and assemblages was relative (i.e. that assemblages are a kind of strata, or vice versa) is clear from the following:

> From this standpoint, we may oppose the consistency of assemblages to the stratification of milieus. But once again, this opposition is only relative, entirely relative. Just as milieus swing between a stratum state and a movement of destratification, assemblages swing between a territorial closure that tends to restratify them and a deterritorializing movement that connects them to the Cosmos. Thus it is not surprising that the distinction we were seeking is not between assemblage and something else, but between two limits of any possible assemblage. (Deleuze and Guattari, *A Thousand Plateaus*, p. 337)

In addition, Deleuze distinguishes between two forms of deterritorialization. The first form, *relative deterritorialization*, refers to processes which destabilize the identity of an assemblage, opening it up to transformations which may yield another identity (in a process called 'reterritorialization'). The second form is quite different, and it is referred to as *absolute deterritorialization*. In this second form it involves a much more radical identity change: indeed, a loss of identity altogether, but without falling into an undifferentiated chaos. Assemblages exist as actual entities, but the structure of the processes of assembly (what gives these processes their recurrent nature, or what explains that they can be repeated in the first place) is not actual but virtual. When deterritorialization is absolute it means that the process has departed from actual reality to reach the virtual dimension. In this sense, the term is synonymous with 'counter-actualization' as the limit process which creates the plane of immanent multiplicities which define the virtual structure of assemblages. The two limits referred to in the quote above are, on the one hand, a highly territorialized and coded assemblage and, on the other, the plane of immanence containing the virtual structure of all assemblages linked by relations of exteriority. In Chapter 2 I discuss the question of the virtual structure of assemblages using the concept of the 'diagram' of an assemblage.

22. Bunge, *Causality and Modern Science*, p. 47.
23. Ibid., p. 178. Bunge credits both Spinoza and Leibniz with the introduction of efficient inner causation. Gilles Deleuze continues this tradition when he gives equal importance to capacities to affect and capacities to be affected.
24. Ibid., 49.
25. Wesley C. Salmon, *Scientific Explanation and the Causal Structure of the World* (Princeton, NJ: Princeton University Press, 1984), pp. 30–34.
26. Bunge, *Causality and Modern Science*, pp. 100–1.
27. R.S. Peters, *The Concept of Motivation* (London: Routledge & Kegan Paul, 1960), p. 29.
28. Max Weber, *The Theory of Social and Economic Organization* (New York: Free Press of Glencoe, 1964), p. 99.
29. The concept of culture I espouse ... is essentially a semiotic one. Believing, with Max Weber, that man is an animal suspended in *webs of significance* he himself has spun, I take culture to be those webs, and the analysis of it to be therefore not an experimental science in search of law but an interpretive one in search of meaning (Clifford Geertz, 'Thick description: toward an interpretive theory of culture', in *The Interpretation of Culture* [New York: Basic Books, 1973], p. 5 [my emphasis])

Geertz goes on to speak of 'structures of signification', as if this expression meant the same thing as 'webs of significance', a manœuvre which illustrates the error I am discussing here. On the other hand, it must be admitted that Geertz's 'thick descriptions' of cultural practices are indeed invaluable as a *starting point* in any social explanation, and this regardless of his rejection of explanatory strategies in favour of descriptive ones.
30. Weber, *Theory of Social and Economic Organization*, p. 91.
31. Ibid., p. 116.
32. Ibid., p. 115. Weber discusses four ideal types of social action: (1) action

oriented towards the matching of means to individually chosen ends; (2) action oriented emotionally; (3) action oriented by habituation to a tradition; and (4) action oriented towards an absolute value, that is, action 'involving a conscious belief in the absolute value of some ethical, aesthetic, religious, or other form of behaviour, entirely for its own sake and independently of any prospects of external success'.

33. Ibid., p. 117.
34. 'Thus causal explanation depends on being able to determine that there is a probability, which in the ideal case can be numerically stated, but is always in some sense calculable, that a given event (overt or subjective) will be followed or accompanied by another event' (ibid., p. 99).

Chapter 2

1. Aristotle, *The Metaphysics* (Buffalo, NY:, Prometheus Books, 1991), p. 155.
2. One is called that which subsists as such according to accident in one way, and in another, that which subsists essentially. A thing is called one according to accident, for instance Coriscus and what is musical, and the musical Coriscus; for it is one and the same thing to say, Coriscus and what is musical, as to say, Coriscus the musician; also, to say the musical and the just is one with saying the just musician Coriscus. For all these are called one according to accident. (Ibid., p. 97)
3. 'The very nature of a thing will not, accordingly, be found in any of those things that are not the species of a genus, but in these only, for these seem to be predicated not according to participation or passion, nor as an accident' (ibid., p. 136).
4. Michael T. Ghiselin, *Metaphysics and the Origin of Species* (Albany, NY: State University of New York, 1997), p. 78.
5. For a full discussion of the ontological and epistemological aspects of phase space, see Manuel DeLanda, *Intensive Science and Virtual Philosophy* (London: Continuum, 2002), Ch. 1.
6. For Deleuze's most extended discussion of diagrams, see Gilles Deleuze, *Foucault* (Minneapolis, MN: University of Minnesota Press, 1988), pp. 34–41 and 71–2.

The structure of a space of possibilities is sometimes referred to as a 'multiplicity', a term that in French is equivalent to 'manifold', the differential geometry spaces used in the construction of phase space. Deleuze sometimes uses the terms 'multiplicity' and 'diagram' as synonyms. Thus, he says that 'every diagram is a spatio-temporal multiplicity' (ibid., p. 34). But he also uses alternative formulations that do not involve the mathematics of phase space. Thus he defines a diagram as a display of relations of force, or of a distribution of capacities to affect and be affected (ibid., pp. 71–2). Since capacities may exist without being exercised (i.e. since they may exist as possibilities) they form a possibility space, and a diagram would display whatever structure this space has. Elsewhere, his definition departs from this spatial form. He argues that unlike an assemblage where the material and expressive roles (or the content and the expression) are clearly distinguished, the diagram of an assemblage involves *unformalized functions and unformed matter*. This means that diagrams have an abstract structure in which the expressive and the material are not differentiated, a differentiation that emerges only when the diagram is divergently actualized in concrete assemblages. One way of thinking about the status of diagrams is, therefore, as the product of a full deterritorialization of a concrete assemblage, since it is the opposite process (territorialization or actualization) that differentiates the material from the expressive. See Gilles Deleuze and Félix Guattari, *A Thousand Plateaus* (Minneapolis, MN: University of Minnesota Press, 1987), p. 142.

Finally, while 'multiplicity' and 'diagram' are sometimes used interchangeably, at other times they refer to separate entities: the structure of a possibility space, on the one hand, and the agency responsible for the absolute deterritorialization, the abstract machine or quasi-causal operator, on the other. For a detailed explanation of these notions and their relations, see DeLanda, *Intensive Science and Virtual Philosophy*, Chs 2 and 3.

7. Because Deleuze does not subscribe to the multiscale social ontology that I am elaborating here, he never says that each of these entities (interpersonal networks, institutional organizations, cities, etc.) have their own diagram. On the contrary, he asserts that the diagram 'is coextensive with the social field' (Deleuze, *Foucault* p. 34). Deleuze gives as examples of 'social fields' contemporary 'disciplinary societies', the 'sovereign societies' that came before them, 'primitive societies', 'feudal societies', etc. (ibid., pp. 34–5). In the social ontology I am presenting there is no such thing as 'society as a whole' or an overall 'social field', so I am breaking in a rather drastic way with Deleuze here.

This implies that the terms 'micro' and 'macro' as used in this book do not correspond to Deleuze's 'molecular' and 'molar'. But some correspondence may still be achieved: at every level of scale we may have, on the one hand, populations of micro-entities, populations characterized by intensive properties such as rates of growth, or the rate at which some components propagate within them; and, on the other hand, some of the members of these populations may be caught into larger macro-entities, regularized and routinized. The entities belonging to the populations could be seen as 'molecular', while the entities caught in the larger aggregates would be 'molar', particularly if the macro-entity is highly territorialized. These remarks soften the differences but do not completely eliminate them. For the molecular and the molar see Deleuze and Guattari, *A Thousand Plateaus*, p. 217.

8. Max Weber, *The Theory of Social and Economic Organization* (New York: Free Press of Glencoe, 1964), pp. 328–60.

9. William Bechtel and Robert C. Richardson, *Discovering Complexity. Decomposition and Localization Strategies in Scientific Thought* (Princeton, NJ: Princeton University Press, 1993), pp. 52–9.

10. Gilles Deleuze, *Logic of Sense* (New York: Columbia University Press, 1990), p. 169. On the other hand Deleuze sometimes writes about diagrams as if they themselves were causes of which assemblages are the effects. Thus he writes that 'the diagram acts as a non-unifying immanent cause ... the cause of the concrete assemblages that execute its relations' (Deleuze, *Foucault*, p. 37).

11.   In the last decade the discipline of sociology resuscitated an old dilemma in a new form – a form, unfortunately, that has done little to resolve the dilemma itself. The perennial conflict between individualistic and collectivistic theories has been reworked as a conflict between micro sociology and macro sociology ... I would like to begin by suggesting that this equation of micro with individual is extremely misleading, as, indeed, is the attempt to find any specific size correlation with the micro–macro difference. There can be no empirical referents for micro or macro as such. They are analytical contrasts, suggesting emergent levels within empirical units, not antagonistic empirical units themselves. (Jeffrey C. Alexander, 'Action and its environments', in Jeffrey C. Alexander, Bernhard Giesen, Richard Münch, Neil J. Smelser [eds], *The Micro–Macro Link*, [Berkeley, CA: University of California Press, 1987], pp. 290–91)
   In the same volume, another sociologist writes:
   A fundamental distinction such as that between micro and macro must be general and analytical, not tied to a fixed case. By this standard, the individual person, household, or firm cannot be treated as intrinsically micro, and the society, nation, or economy as unalterably macro. Rather, designations of micro and macro are relative to each other and, in particular, to the analytic purpose at hand. The overall status or role of a given family member (ego) may be macro relative to ego's relation to a certain kin group member, but micro relative to the status or role of ego's lineage in a marriage exchange system; the marriage system in turn may be micro relative to a mythic cycle. The job satisfaction of a worker may be macro relative to the psychological stress on his or her children, but micro relative to the quality of his or her job. That in turn may be micro relative to the morale or efficiency of the factory or branch office, which is micro relative to the financial condition of the corporation, which is micro relative to the competitiveness of the industry or the business cycle of the national or international economy – which are, however,

micro relative to the ideological spirit of the age. (Dean R. Gerstein, 'To unpack micro and macro: link small with large and part with whole', ibid., p. 88)

12. Roy Bhaskar, *A Realist Theory of Science* (London: Verso, 1997), p. 114. While Bhaskar's realism comes very close to Deleuze's in some aspects it is incompatible with it because Bhaskar is a self-declared essentialist. As he writes:

In general to classify a group of things together in science, to call them by the same name, presupposes that they possess a real essence or nature in common, though it does not presuppose that the real essence or nature is known ... A chemist will classify diamonds, graphite and black carbon together because he believes that they possess a real essence in common, which may be identified as the atomic (or electronic) structure of carbon. (Ibid., p. 210)

13. Peter Hedström and Richard Swedberg, 'Social mechanisms: an introductory essay', in *Social Mechanisms. An Analytical Approach to Social Theory*, (eds) Peter Hedström and Richard Swedberg (Cambridge: Cambridge University Press, 1998), pp. 22–3. The authors propose three different types of mechanism: macro–micro, micro–micro and micro–macro. The first type would figure in explanations of the relations between a social situation involving large sociological phenomena (such as the distribution of income or power in a population) and individual social actors. The large-scale process may, for example, create different opportunities and risks for different actors, who must include these opportunities and risks as part of their reasons to act. The second type refers mainly to social–psychological mechanisms, that is, to the mental processes explaining the making of particular decisions (in the case of motives) or to the processes behind the formation of habits, the production of emotions or the acquisition of beliefs (in the case of reasons). Finally, the third type refers to mechanisms governing the interactions among individual actors which generate collective outcomes.

The problem is that the terms 'micro' and 'macro' are used in their absolute sense, with 'micro' referring to individual persons and 'macro' designating society as a whole. But in assemblage theory the distinction between micro- and macro-levels is relative to scale. Relativizing the distinction implies that their third type of mechanism, micro–micro, can be eliminated since at any given scale it reduces to the micro–macro one *at the immediately smaller scale*. And similarly for what we may term macro–macro mechanisms. When 'macro' refers to 'total society' there is no need to consider the interactions between wholes. But once the distinction is relativized we do need to consider that wholes made out of individual persons, such as interpersonal networks or institutional organizations, may interact with one another as wholes. The term macro–macro, however, is not necessary, since it reduces to the micro–macro case *at the immediately larger scale*.

14. Mark Granovetter, *Getting a Job: A Study of Contacts and Careers* (Chicago, IL: University of Chicago Press, 1995).

15. David Krackhardt, 'The strength of strong ties: the importance of philos in organizations', in *Networks and Organizations*, (eds) Nitin Nohria and Robert G. Eccles (Boston, MA: Harvard Business School Press, 1992), pp. 218–19.

16. Fernand Braudel, *The Wheels of Commerce* (New York: Harper & Row, 1979), p. 30.

17. When exactly in the history of Europe prices began to be determined impersonally, as opposed to through the decisions of feudal lords, is a controversial point. Braudel argues that all 'the evidence relating to prices as early as the twelfth century indicates that they were already fluctuating, evidence that by then "modern" markets existed and might occasionally be linked together in embryonic, town-to-town networks' (ibid., p. 28).

18. Alan Garfinkel, *Forms of Explanation* (New Haven, CT: Yale University Press, 1981), pp. 58–62.

19. As the sociologist Anthony Giddens argues, unlike the components of a physical entity with emergent properties (such as bronze, a metallic alloy having properties that are more than the sum of the properties of its parts, copper, tin and sometimes lead), the parts of a social assemblage seldom come in pure form. It is easy to imagine the component parts of bronze as existing separately prior to their coming together and forming an alloy, 'but human actors, as recognizable competent agents, do not exist in separation from one another as copper, tin, and lead do. They do not come together *ex nihilo* to form a new entity by their fusion or association' (Anthony Giddens, *The Constitution of Society* [Berkeley, CA: University of California Press, 1986], pp. 171–2).

    Giddens is thus correct in criticizing the limited concept of emergence that implies only to originary emergence. But he is wrong in thinking that giving up this conception implies surrendering the part-to-whole relation in favour of a seamless web. The example of bronze was used by Emile Durkheim to argue for the existence of social emergent properties. See Emile Durkheim, *The Rules of Sociological Method* (New York: The Free Press, 1982), p. 39.

20. Paul DiMaggio, 'Nadel's paradox revisited: relational and cultural aspects of organizational structure', in *Networks and Organizations*, p. 132.

21. Jeffrey L. Pressman and Aaron Wildavsky, *Implementation* (Berkeley, CA: University of California Press, 1984), p. 92.

22. This ability to operate across scales is particularly surprising, given that both genetic and linguistic materials are 'more micro' than any of the entities of which they form a part. But Deleuze and Guattari see this 'molecularization' of expression as precisely what gives genes and words their ability to

produce more complex relations between the micro and the macro. See Deleuze and Guattari, *A Thousand Plateaus*, p. 59.

23. Peter L. Berger and Thomas Luckmann, *The Social Construction of Reality* (New York: Anchor Books, 1967).

Chapter 3

1. 'All the perceptions of the human mind resolve themselves into two kinds, which I shall call IMPRESSIONS and IDEAS. The difference betwixt them consists in the degrees of force and liveliness with which they strike upon the mind, and make their way into our thought and consciousness. Those perceptions, which enter with the most force and violence, we may name *impressions*; and under this name I comprehend all our sensations, passions and emotions, as they make their first appearance in the soul. By *ideas* I mean the faint images of these in thinking and reasoning ...' (David Hume, *A Treatise of Human Nature* [London: Penguin, 1969], p. 49. [emphasis in the original])

2. Ibid., p. 462.

3. Hume, in fact, makes a distinction between relations which may change without changing the related ideas (contiguity, identity, causality) and those in which this is not the case (resemblance, contrariety, degrees of quality and proportions of quantity) (ibid., pp. 117–18). This would seem to contradict the statement that all links between ideas are relations of exteriority. Yet, as Deleuze argues, this is not so. The four relations which do seem to depend on ideas imply a comparison, that is, an operation which is exterior to the ideas being compared. See Gilles Deleuze, *Empiricism and Subjectivity* (New York: Columbia University Press, 1991), pp. 99–101.

4. Hume, *A Treatise of Human Nature*, p. 60.

5. As Deleuze puts it:

   ... if the principles of association explain that ideas are associated, only the principles of the passions can explain that a particular idea, rather than another, is associated at a given moment ... Everything takes place as if the principles of association provided the subject with its necessary form, whereas the principles of the passions provided it with its singular content. (Deleuze, *Empiricism and Subjectivity*, pp. 103–4)

6. Ibid., p. 98. Deleuze is here contrasting an 'assemblage or collection' with a 'system'. This is similar to the contrast he draws in his latter work between 'assemblages' and 'strata'. As I argued in Chapter 1, I prefer to deal with this contrast not as a dichotomy between two types but as a third dimension characterizing assemblages, with highly coded assemblages being 'strata'.

7. Hume, *A Treatise of Human Nature*, p. 327.

8. Ibid., p. 51.

9. Ibid., p. 308.
10. On the effects of madness see ibid., p. 172.
11. Ibid., p. 308.
12. The most famous critique of the combinatorial poverty of associationism is Jerry A. Fodor and Zenon W. Pylyshyn, 'Connectionism and cognitive architecture: a critical analysis', in John Haugeland (ed.), *Mind Design II. Philosophy, Psychology and Artificial Intelligence* (Cambridge, MA: MIT Press, 1997), pp. 309–50.

    For a discussion of recent associationist extensions that may compensate for this poverty see William Bechtel and Adele Abrahamsen, *Connectionism and the Mind. An Introduction to Parallel Distributed Processing in Networks* (Cambridge, MA, and Oxford: Basil Blackwell, 1991), pp. 101–2; Andy Clark, *Microcognition. Philosophy, Cognitive Science, and Parallel Distributed Processing* (Cambridge, MA: MIT Press, 1990), pp. 143–51.
13. A theory of grammar that meets both the combinatorial productivity requirement as well as the evolutionary one is Zellig Harris, *A Theory of Language and Information: A Mathematical Approach* (Oxford: Clarendon Press, 1981). I give a fully evolutionary history of real languages and dialects, based on Zellig Harris's ideas, in Manuel DeLanda, *A Thousand Years of Nonlinear History* (New York: Zone Books, 1997), Ch. 3.
14. Hume, *A Treatise of Human Nature*, p. 144. A belief 'can only bestow on our ideas an additional force or vivacity'.
15. Ibid., p. 146.
16. Ervin Goffman, *Interaction Ritual. Essays on Face-to-Face Behaviour* (New York: Pantheon Books, 1967), p. 1 (my italics).
17. Ibid., p. 19.
18. Ibid., p. 103.
19. Ibid., p. 34.
20. Ibid., p. 103.
21. Analytical philosophers, for decades infatuated with syntax and semantics, are beginning to turn around and include this pragmatic dimension. Thus, Ian Hacking, in his analysis of the term 'social construction', deliberately resists asking the question 'what is its semantic content?' and asks instead 'what is its point?' (i.e. what is its significance?) See Ian Hacking, *The Social Construction of What?* (Cambridge, MA: Harvard University Press, 2000), p. 5.

    An argument that questions of significance are not the same as questions of signification can be found in Denis C. Phillips, *Philosophy, Science, and Social Inquiry* (Oxford: Pergamon Press, 1987), p. 109.
22. Goffman, *Interaction Ritual*, pp. 162–4.
23. Ibid., pp. 218–19.
24. John Scott, *Social Network Analysis* (London: Sage Publications, 2000), pp. 11, 31 and 75.

25. Ibid., pp. 70–73.
26. Ibid., p. 12.
27. Ibid., p. 79. See also Graham Crow, *Social Solidarities* (Buckingham: Open University Press, 2002), pp. 52–3.
28. Crow, *Social Solidarities*, pp. 119–20.
29. On local dialects as badges of identity see William Labov, 'The social setting of linguistic change', in *Sociolinguistic Patterns* (Philadelphia, PN: University of Pennsylvania Press, 1972), p. 271.
30. Crow, *Social Solidarities*, pp. 128–9.
31. Ibid., pp. 86–8.
32. Charles Tilly, *Stories, Identities, and Political Change* (Lanham, MD: Rowman & Littlefield, 2002), pp. 28–9.
33. Charles Tilly, *Durable Inequality* (Berkeley, CA: University of California Press, 1999), p. 66.
34. Gilles Deleuze and Félix Guattari, *Anti-Oedipus* (Minneapolis, MN: University of Minnesota Press), pp. 147, 155.
35. Tilly, *Stories, Identities, and Political Change*, p. 12. Tilly is perhaps the most coherent advocate of realism in social theory today although his fear of essences has made him espouse a rather watered-down version of it. He declares himself to be a 'relational realist', that is, someone who believes in the mind-independent existence of relations but not of the entities that enter into relations, although he grudgingly acknowledges the existence of human beings with physiological needs. Enduring entities, in his account, presuppose essences and are thus less worthy of commitment. As he puts it, social explanations can be either in terms of essences or in terms of bonds. See Tilly, *Durable Inequality*, p. 45.

But, first of all, a commitment to entities need not involve essences at all if the entities are accounted for by the historical process that produced them. Secondly, although social interaction is indeed relational, in the sense that the capacities exercised by the social actors are not reducible to the actors' defining properties, capacities do depend on the existence of these enduring properties, and thus, on the existence of enduring entities. Finally, to subordinate entities to relations comes dangerously close to a commitment to relations of interiority, that is, to wholes in which the parts are constituted by the very relations which yield the whole.
36. Ibid., p. 90.
37. Ibid., p. 54.
38. Ibid., p. 89.
39. Ibid., pp. 106–7.
40. Ibid., pp. 52–3.
41. Ibid., pp. 105–6.
42. Tilly, *Stories, Identities, and Political Change*, 102–3.

43.   No general population larger than a local community ever maintains a coherent system of stratification in a strong sense of the word; even the so-called caste systems of India accommodated great variation in rank orders from village to village. In general, rank orders remain inconsistent, apparent strata contain considerable heterogeneity, and mobility blurs dividing lines. (Ibid., pp. 28–9)

44.   The idea of difference, or gap, is at the basis of the very notion of *space*, that is, a set of distinct and coexisting positions which are exterior to one another and which are defined in relation to one another through their *mutual exteriority* and their relations of proximity, vicinity, or distance, as well as through relations of order, such as above, below, or *between*. Certain properties of members of the petit-bourgeoise can, for example, be deduced from the fact that they occupy an intermediate position between two extreme positions, without being objectively identifiable or subjectively identified with one or the other position. (Pierre Bourdieu, *Practical Reason* ([Standford, 1998], CA: Stanford University Press, p. 6 [emphasis in the original])

45. Pierre Bourdieu, *The Logic of Practice* (Cambridge: Polity Press, 1990), p. 54 (my italics).

46. Ibid., p. 55. A more generous reading of the habitus, along assemblage theory lines, would be as the topological diagram of the set of habits and routines that make up individual persons, that is, as the structure of the space of possibilities for different combinations of habits and skills.

47. 'So far as the social world is concerned, the neo-Kantian theory, which gives language and, more generally, representations a specifically symbolic efficacy in the construction of reality, is perfectly justified. By structuring the perception that social agents have of the social world, the act of naming helps to establish the structure of this world' (Pierre Bourdieu, *Language and Symbolic Power* [Cambridge: Harvard University Press, 1991], p. 105).

48. Tilly, *Durable Inequality*, p. 76.

49. Ibid., p. 36.

Chapter 4

1. Max Weber, *The Theory of Social and Economic Organization* (New York: Free Press of Glencoe, 1964), p. 331.

2. Ibid., pp. 328–36.

3. Ibid., p. 348.

4. Ibid., p. 359.

5. As Weber puts it, even in the most rational bureaucracy the very 'belief in legality comes to be established and habitual and this means it is partly traditional' (ibid., p. 382).

6. James S. Coleman, *Foundations of Social Theory* (Cambridge, MA: Belknap Press, 2000), p. 66.

7. A sick worker must be treated by a doctor using accepted medical procedures; whether the worker is treated effectively is less important. A bus company must service required routes whether or not there are many passengers. A university must maintain appropriate departments independent of the departments' enrollment. Activity, that is, has ritual significance: it maintains appearances and validates an organization. (John W. Meyer and Brian Rowan, 'Institutionalized organizations: formal structure as myth and ceremony', in Walter W. Powell and Paul J. MiMaggio [eds], *The New Institutionalism in Organizational Analysis* [Chicago, IL: University of Chicago Press, 1991], p. 55)

8. W. Richard Scott and John W. Meyer, 'The organization of societal sectors: propositions and early evidence', in Powell and DiMaggio (eds), *The New Institutionalism in Organizational Analysis*, p. 124. Valuable as this neo-institutional work in sociology may be it is fatally flawed in one sense: it relies on social constructivism and its idealist ontology. Hence, despite the apparent recognition that there are real technical questions involved in the operation of some organizations, ultimately what 'counts as technical' is just a mere convention, that is, a matter of definition, an assertion which makes the distinction between technical and ceremonial factors useless.

9. Michel Foucault, *Discipline and Punish. The Birth of Prison* (New York: Vintage Books, 1979), p. 169.

10. Ibid., p. 171.

11. Ibid., p. 153.

12. Ibid., pp. 195–6.

13. Ibid., pp. 191–2.

14. Ibid., p. 190.

15. Weber, *The Theory of Social and Economic Organization*, p. 363.

16. In Deleuze's application of assemblage analysis to Foucault's work, he singles out the buildings of hospitals and prisons as the material components (or as the 'form of content') and the discourses of medicine or criminology as the expressive components (or the 'form of expression'). See Gilles Deleuze, *Foucault* (Minneapolis, MN: University of Minnesota Press, 1988), p. 62.

17. Jeffrey Pfeffer and Gerald R. Salancik, *The External Control of Organizations. A Resource Dependence Perspective* (Stanford, CA: Stanford University Press, 2003), p. 46.

18. Ibid., pp. 48–50.

19. Ibid., p. 51. Despite these useful insights there is a major shortcoming to the theory of resource dependence. The authors' reliance on social constructivism to think about the way in which an organization (or rather, its administrative staff) 'perceives' its relations with other organizations leads

them to the idealist conclusion that an organization's environment is created by those relations to which it actually pays attention. As they put it: 'Noting that an organization's environment is enacted, or created by attentional processes, tends to shift the focus from characteristics of the objective environment to characteristics of the decision process by which organizations select and ignore information' (ibid., p. 74). But why would anyone want to shift attention away from the objective distribution of opportunities and risks that an environment affords an organization? It is only by preserving the distinction between real opportunities to acquire resources (or real risks of losing autonomy) and the awareness that an organization may or may not have of them, that one can speak of 'missed opportunities' (or of 'underestimated risks') and of the effects that such mistaken evaluations may have on an organization's ability to cope with real dependencies. The notion of an 'enacted environment' is, in fact, quite useless, but the fact that the social constructivist part of the theory of resource dependence can be so easily separated from the rest shows that its role is mostly ceremonial rather than technical.

20. Ibid., Ch. 6.
21. Walter W. Powell, 'Neither market nor Hierarchy. Network forms of organization', in Michael Handel (ed.), *The Sociology of Organizations* (Thousand Oaks, CA: Sage, 2003), p. 326.
22. John R. Munkirs and James I. Sturgeon, 'Oligopolistic cooperation: conceptual and empirical evidence of market structure evolution', in Marc R. Tool and Warren J. Samuels (eds), *The Economy as a System of Power* (New Brunswick, NJ: Transaction Press, 1989).
23. Paul M. Hohenberg and Lynn Hollen Lees, *The Making of Urban Europe 1000–1950* (Cambridge, MA: Harvard University Press, 1985), p. 202.
24. Michael Best, *The New Competition* (Cambridge, MA: Harvard University Press, 1990), pp. 14–15.
25. Ibid., p. 205.
26. Annalee Saxenian, *Regional Advantage. Culture and Competition in Silicon Valley and Route 128* (Cambridge, MA: Harvard University Press, 1996), pp. 2–3.
27. Pfeffer and Salancik, *The External Control of Organizations*, pp. 94–5.
28. Best, *The New Competition*, pp. 239–40.
29. Howard T. Odum and Elizabeth C. Odum, *Energy Basis for Man and Nature* (New York: McGraw-Hill, 1981), p. 41.
30. Saxenian, *Regional Advantage*, pp. 34–6.
31. Pfeffer and Salancik, *The External Control of Organizations*, pp. 178–9.
32. Walter W. Powell and Paul J. DiMaggio 'The iron cage revisited: institutional isomorphism and collective rationality in organizational fields', in Powell and DiMaggio (eds), *The New Institutionalism in Organizational Analysis*, pp. 71–2.

33. Michael T. Hannan and John Freeman, *Organizational Ecology* (Cambridge, MA: Harvard University Press, 1989), p. 66.

34. Oliver E. Williamson, 'Transaction cost economics and organization theory', in Oliver E. Williamson (ed.), *Organization Theory* (New York: Oxford University Press, 1995), p. 223.

35. Oliver E. Williamson, 'Chester Barnard and the incipient science of organization', ibid., p. 196.

The focus of neo-institutional economists is at times too narrow (the only choice being between making or buying, or between internal hierarchies and external markets) so it does not cover all the possible resource interdependencies that may arise. In particular, division of labour among organizations of similar size (that is, in the absence of clear-cut domination by a much larger firm) may lead to specialization on products or activities which are dissimilar but closely complementary. This, in turn, presents firms with another choice, not to make or buy but to make or cooperate. The resulting interdependencies may lead to alliances or partnerships based on contracts for the transfer, exchange or pooling of technologies, standards and even personnel. See G.B. Richardson, 'The organization of industry', in Peter J. Buckley and Jonathan Michie (eds), *Firms, Organizations and Contracts* (Oxford: Oxford University Press, 2001), pp. 59–63.

36. Terry M. Moe, 'The politics of structural choice: toward a theory of public bureaucracy', in *Organization Theory*, p. 125.

37. Best, *The New Competition*, p. 82.

38. Jeffrey L. Pressman and Aaron Wildavsky, *Implementation* (Berkeley, CA: University of California Press, 1984), Ch. 5.

39. Daniel A. Mazmanian and Paul A. Sabatier, *Implementation and Public Policy* (Lanham, MD: University Press of America, 1989), p. 9.

40. B. Dan Wood and Richard W. Waterman, *Bureaucratic Dynamics* (Boulder, CO: Westview Press, 1994), pp. 22–30.

41. Pfeffer and Salancik, *The External Control of Organizations*, pp. 210–11.

42. Charles Tilly, *Stories, Identities, and Political Change* (Lanham, MD: Rowman & Littlefield, 2002), p. 13.

43. Hannu Nurmi, *Comparing Voting Systems* (Dordrecht: D. Reidel, 1987), pp. 2–3.

44. James O. Freedman, *Crisis and Legitimacy. The Administrative Process and American Government* (Cambridge: Cambridge University Press, 1978), pp. 16–19.

45. Ibid., pp. 44–6.

46. Ibid., pp. 129–30 and 161–76.

47. Wood and Waterman, *Bureaucratic Dynamics* pp. 33–7.

48. Ibid., p. 144.

49. Rolf Torstendahl, *Bureaucratization in Northwestern Europe, 1880–1985* (London: Routledge, 1991), pp. 203–16.

50. David Sanders, *Patterns of Political Instability* (London: Macmillan, 1981), pp. 5–10.
51. While some discrepancy between statutory objectives and policy decisions is almost inevitable (if for no other reason than disagreements about how general rules apply to specific cases), such differences can be reduced if the statute stipulates unambiguous objectives, assigns implementation to sympathetic agencies who will give it high priority, minimizes the number of veto points and provides sufficient incentives (such as subsidies or compensatory changes in unrelated policies) to overcome recalcitrant officials, provides sufficient financial resources to conduct the technical analyses and process individual cases, and biases the decision rules and access points in favour of programme objectives. (Mazmanian and Sabatier, *Implementation and Public Policy*, p. 36)
52. Douglass C. North, *Institutions, Institutional Change and Economic Performance* (New York: Cambridge University Press, 1995), pp. 120–31.
53. Tilly, *Stories, Identities, and Political Change*, p. 129.
54. T.K. Oommen, *Citizenship, Nationality, and Ethnicity* (Cambridge: Polity Press, 1997). See p. 34 for the difference between state-led and state-seeking nationalisms and pp. 135–45 for mixtures in concrete cases.
55. Charles Tilly, *Big Structures, Large Processes, Huge Comparisons* (New York: Russell Sage Foundation, 1984), pp. 103–11.

Chapter 5

1. Robert E. Park, 'The city: suggestions for investigation of human behaviour in the urban environment', in Robert E. Park and Ernest W. Burgess (eds), *The City* (Chicago, IL: University of Chicago Press, 1984), pp. 4–6.
2. Anthony Giddens, *The Constitution of Society* (Berkeley, CA: University of California Press, 1986), pp. 118–19. Giddens' treatment of regionalized locales is similar to Deleuze and Guattari's concept of a territory: a concept they develop in relation to animal territories but that is not confined to this example. To see the parallel, we must add to Giddens' definition in terms of rhythmic or periodic routines the expressive marking of boundaries. A territory is, in this sense, 'an act of rhythm that has become expressive'.

   Cf. Gilles Deleuze and Félix Guattari, *A Thousand Plateaus* (Minneapolis, MN: University of Minnesota Press, 1987), p. 315. Actually, there are three elements in the definition of a territorial assemblage. One needs 'a block of space–time constituted by the periodic repetition of [a] component' (ibid., p. 313) made into a territory by marking its boundaries, drawing 'a circle around that uncertain and fragile centre, to organize a limited space' (ibid., p. 311). And, in addition to rhythm and boundary, there must be the possibility of opening up the circle, of venturing away from home through a gap in the border. This, of course, corresponds to the processes of deterritorialization which can open up an assemblage to future possibilities or even change its identity.

3. Fernand Braudel, *The Structures of Everyday Life* (Berkeley, CA: University of California Press, 1992), p. 267.

4. James E. Vance Jr, *The Continuing City. Urban Morphology in Western Civilization* (Baltimore, MD: Johns Hopkins University Press, 1990), pp. 24–5.

5. Braudel, *The Structures of Everyday Life*, p. 308.

6. Vance Jr, *The Continuing City*, p. 416.

7. Ibid., p. 378.

8. Braudel, *The Structures of Everyday Life*, p. 310.

9. Ibid., p. 317.

10. Ibid., p. 324.

11. Michel Foucault, *Discipline and Punish. The Birth of Prison* (New York: Vintage Books, 1979), p. 172.

12. Giddens, *The Constitution of Society*, p. 152.

13. Vance Jr, *The Continuing City*, p. 175.

14. Ibid., pp. 120 and 184–5. 'The central morphological truth learned in the bastides was that inter accessible and proportionate layout of the town is one of the more concrete expressions of functional equality, and a strong bulwark in its defense' (ibid., p. 200).

15. Ibid., pp. 36–7.

16. As the economist Thomas Shelling has shown, the dynamics behind these processes are those of people responding to an environment which consists of people responding to each other: given a group of people's preferences to live in proximity to similar groups, each decision made to move into or out of a neighbourhood will change the neighbourhood itself, influencing the future decisions of current residents and of people wanting residence there. See Thomas C. Schelling, *Micromotives and Macrobehaviour* (New York: Norton, 1978), Ch. 4.

17. Robert E. Park, 'The city', in Park and Burgess, *The City*, p. 9.

18. Vance Jr, *The Continuing City*, p. 316.

19. Ernest W. Burgess, 'The growth of the city', in Park and Burgess, *The City*, p. 50.

20. Paul M. Hohenberg and Lynn Hollen Lees, *The Making of Urban Europe 1000–1950* (Cambridge, MA: Harvard University Press, 1985), p. 299.

21. Vance Jr, *The Continuing City*, p. 409.

22. Ibid., pp. 412–13.

23. Ibid., pp. 74–7.

24. Braudel, *The Structures of Everyday Life*, pp. 484–9.

25. Ibid., p. 486.

26. Masahisa Fujita, Paul Krugman and Anthony J. Venables, *The Spatial*

Economy. Cities, Regions, and International Trade (Cambridge, MA: MIT Press, 1999), p. 4. See also Peter M. Allen, *Cities and Regions as Self-Organizing Systems* (Amsterdam: Gordon & Breach, 1997), p. 27.

27. Vance Jr, *The Continuing City*, p. 373.

28. Deleuze and Guattari view rhythmically repeated motifs and the counter-points they create with the external milieu as the two ways in which expressive components self-organize in territorial assemblages, including animal assemblages, transforming what was mere signature into a style. See Deleuze and Guattari, *A Thousand Plateaus*, p. 317.

29. Spiro Kostoff, *The City Shaped. Urban Patterns and Meanings throughout History* (London: Bullfinch Press, 1991), pp. 284–5.

30. Vance Jr, *The Continuing City*, p. 56.

31. Braudel, *The Structures of Everyday Life*, p. 512.

32. Vance Jr, *The Continuing City*, pp. 502–4.

33. Hohenberg and Hollen Lees, *The Making of Urban Europe*, pp. 20–23 (for the period between the years 1000 and 1300); pp. 106–7 (1500–1800); and pp. 217–220 (1800–1900).

34. Fujita *et al.*, *The Spatial Economy*, p. 34.

35. Allen, *Cities and Regions as Self-Organizing Systems*, p. 53.

36. Hohenberg and Hollen Lees, *The Making of Urban Europe*, pp. 51–4.

37. Ibid., p. 240.

38. Fernand Braudel, *The Perspective of the World* (New York: Harper & Row, 1979), pp. 27–31.

39. Hohenberg and Hollen Lees, *The Making of Urban Europe*, p. 66.

40. Braudel, *The Perspective of the World*, pp. 30–31.

41. Hohenberg and Hollen Lees, *The Making of Urban Europe*, p. 6.

42. Ibid., p. 281.

43. Paul Kennedy, *The Rise and Fall of the Great Powers. Economic Change and Military Conflict from 1500 to 2000* (New York: Random House, 1987), pp. 70–71.

44. J. Craig Barker, *International Law and International Relations* (London: Continuum, 2000), pp. 5–8. For the five-year negotiation period see Geoffrey Parker, *The Thirty Years' War* (London: Routledge & Kegan Paul, 1987), pp. 170–78.

45. Kennedy, *The Rise and Fall of the Great Powers*, p. 86 (emphasis in the original).

46. Fernand Braudel, *The Wheels of Commerce* (New York: Harper & Row, 1979), pp. 544–5.

47. Ibid., p. 525 (my emphasis).

48. Braudel, *The Structures of Everyday Life*, p. 527.

49. Hohenberg and Hollen Lees, *The Making of Urban Europe*, p. 242.

50. Kostoff, *The City Shaped*, pp. 211–15.

51. Ibid., p. 217.

52. I attempted to synthesize all available materials on the political history of languages and dialects in Manuel DeLanda, *A Thousand Years of Nonlinear History* (New York: Zone Books, 1997), Ch. 3.

53. Christopher Duffy, *The Fortress in the Age of Vauban and Frederick the Great* (London: Routledge & Kegan Paul, 1985), p. 87.

54. Peter J. Taylor, *Political Geography* (New York: Longman, 1985), pp. 113–15.

55. Braudel introduced the term 'world-economy' to discuss the Mediterranean as a coherent economic area in Fernand Braudel, *The Mediterranean. And the Mediterranean World in the Age of Philip II*, Vol. 1. (Berkeley, CA: University of California Press, 1995), p. 419. Braudel attributes the original concept to two German scholars in Braudel, *The Perspective of the World*, p. 634, n. 4.

56. Immanuel Wallerstein, *World-Systems Analysis. An Introduction* (Durham, NC: Duke University Press, 2004), pp. 11–17.

57. Ibid., p. 16. Wallerstein's macro-reductionism derives directly from his use of Hegelian totalities to conceptualize large-scale social entities. See Immanuel Wallerstein, *The Capitalist World-Economy* (Cambridge: Cambridge University Press, 1993), p. 4.

58. Braudel, *The Wheels of Commerce*, p. 458.

Index